How To Meet The Queen

Ask Good Questions - Get Good Answers

Albert Lee

Nilwall Group Inc.
Toronto, Canada

Copyright © 2012 Nilwall Group Inc.
All rights reserved.
Printed in the United States of America
First Edition
ISBN 978-0-9880406-0-1

APT is a trademark of Nilwall Group Inc. All other trademarks are the property of their respective owners.

No part of this publication may be reproduced, stored in or introduced into a retrieval system, or transmitted, in any form, or by any means (electronic, mechanical, photocopying, recording, or otherwise), without prior permission. Requests for permission should be directed to info@6basix.com.

Library and Archives Canada Cataloguing in Publication

Lee, Albert, 1959-
    How to meet the queen : ask good questions- get good answers / Albert Lee.

Includes bibliographical references.
ISBN 978-0-9880406-0-1

    1. Interviewing. 2. Interviews. 3. Questions and answers. I. Title.

BF637.I5L44 2012   158.3'9   C2012-903350-2

Contents

Acknowledgements v
1. The Importance Of Observation 1
2. The Secret Sauce 15
3. Attitude – Be Curious 23
4. Attitude – Be Creative 35
5. Attitude – Be Persistent 53
6. Attitude – Be Thorough 63
7. Attitude – Be Skeptical 77
8. Preparation – Have A Specific Objective 93
9. Preparation – Do Your Homework 107
10. Preparation – Know Your Audience 115
11. Preparation – Choose The Right Person 125
12. Preparation – Don't Assume 141
13. Technique – Watch Your Language 155
14. Technique – Listen Actively 169
15. Technique – Soften Up Your Audience 183
16. Technique – Ask Short Simple Questions 193
17. Technique – Look For Inconsistencies 205
18. Jump Start With Attributes 211
19. Improving Your APT-itude 239
20. Putting It All Together 243
Epilogue - What Happened With The Queen 259
Bibliography 263
About The Author 273

ACKNOWLEDGEMENTS

Through trial-by-fire I learned a great deal about the software industry alongside my trusting colleagues connected with xkoto Inc. and SWI Group over the last twenty-five years.

In all that time, my wife, Evelyn, later bolstered by our sons Jordan and Justin, endured the tumult by my side.

This book is the outcome of their unquestioning support.

Chapter 1

THE IMPORTANCE OF OBSERVATION

All Roads Lead To The Queen

Three miles – that's about as close as I ever came to Queen Elizabeth II (approximately five kilometres for you metric types). Her Majesty visited downtown Toronto in 2002 while I was in my midtown office, quite oblivious to all the pomp and circumstance swirling around the Monarch.

Yet in retrospect, the Queen had always been a part of my life. In primary school we began our days singing "God Save The *Queen*" (this was before the adoption of "O Canada" as the national anthem). My middle school was located on *Queen* St. I had a rare stamp collection crammed full of portraits of a youthful *Queen* that I one day foolishly gave away in a fit of insanity. I was accepted for post-graduate studies at *Queen's* University. When I wasn't working in midtown I was commuting every day on the *QEW* Highway – guess what the "QE" in "QEW" stands for?

Nevertheless, all things royal held no special place for me until about a year ago. The book you now hold is my journal of a year-long quest to find a way to meet with the Queen. Was this the consequence of some bet gone wrong? No. My leave of good judgement is limited to giving away priceless stamp collections.

The quest for the Queen was self-imposed. I wanted to prove a point – that if you learn to observe by asking good questions – the right questions – you can aim for the impossible, which pretty much sums up the chances for a "commoner" like me to rate an appointment with the Queen.

This book will encourage, entertain, and most of all equip you to ask better questions in every circumstance. While there are other authors you can consult on this subject, the content to follow has three distinctions:

1. I have researched the experts in the "question-asking business" – celebrity interviewers, medical doctors, lawyers, police investigators, even criminals – to extract the real principles that work for them and will work for you.
2. These principles are applied in real-life scenarios, with a particular emphasis on the business world where the returns can be significant.
3. In fifteen successive chapters, I illustrate how each principle works by recounting the actual results from applying the principle in my ongoing pursuit of the Queen. If nothing else, you will enjoy the unfolding tale as we take a glimpse into royal life.

My Initial Steps

It was not natural for me to become a royal watcher as an Asian kid growing up in a mostly white, medium-sized city. Instead, I nurtured a natural curiosity with numbers. Nineteen for example. That was the number of steps from street level up to the second floor dining room in the family restaurant that my father and his siblings ruled for over forty years since before the Second World War. The *Pagoda Chop Suey House* was like most Chinese restaurants of its day – modest looking, and serving up what North Americans considered "authentic" cuisine – sweet and sour chicken balls, egg rolls, fried rice, and of course, chop suey.

Not only did the Pagoda meet local menu expectations, it also met decor expectations - you visit Chinese restaurants for the food, not a good-looking dining room. On one occasion, nineteen steps later, an older patron summited the stairs, paused for breath, and surveyed the tacky paper lanterns, the horseshoe-shaped coat hooks fixed to yellowing walls, and the worn linoleum floor, whereupon he loudly announced that nothing had changed since the War – sadly, the same could not be said of him!

I do not know why I remembered the nineteen steps, but those numerical details would come in handy, but more about that later. This book is not about my obsession with counting but about how we can each make better observations in living life by asking good questions.

Can You Relate?

How observant are you? When you pick a check-out line at the supermarket do you always seem to end up in the longest line? Perhaps you spotted a queue with fewer people but neglected to factor in how loaded the shopping carts were ahead of you. Or maybe you spied no carts ahead of you at all, but then became mired behind someone waiting for a price check on tomato soup. Being unobservant at the store is just a symptom of something worse.

See if you can relate to any of these scenarios:

- **Telemarketing**: You are at home after a long day at work or school and inevitably just as you sit down to dinner the phone rings – why is it always at dinner time (one of the universities in town has been calling me faithfully daily for the past three years)? Of course you have "call display" precisely so you can screen out telemarketers. But telemarketers block their numbers from being displayed precisely so you cannot tell who's calling! Do you pick it up? It could be a call from your mother - or it could be your mother-in-law. Decisions, decisions. Overcome by curiosity, you pick up the phone and ... it's neither – just apparent silence. What now?

    You should hang up immediately, otherwise, the moment you utter a sound, you'll hear a "click" and then your dinner will freeze over as a telemarketer comes on the line to pitch you a Hawaiian cruise or some new credit card.

    You see, *observant* people know that telemarketers use automated dialling systems to "spam" every consumer in the phone directory. As soon as these systems detect a real live person on the other end, they connect the victim to one of those "operators-standing-by". If you want to resume your dinner, you should hang up the moment you detect that long silence.

- **Cyber Crime**: Dinner is now over and you plunk yourself down on your favourite comfy chair and start surfing the Internet. You make your way through the thirty messages waiting in your email inbox and find one apparently from your bank informing you that there's been fraudulent use of your chequing account and directing you to a website to verify your personal information. You wouldn't fall for that, would you?

You are savvy to the ways of the world ... but what harm would there be in just clicking on that web link? If you are *observant*, you would delete that email immediately and inform your bank (by telephone or in person).

Otherwise, you may have just infected your computer or triggered some dormant program to attack a major website. And how did this so-called "malware" infect your computer in the first place? *You* put it there. The software was downloaded the last time you fell for a similar "cyber scam". Malicious software is rampant on the Internet to prey on unobservant victims.

These are just two examples of the dangers of poor observation. On the other hand, learning to observe by asking good questions will equip you to make better decisions and to simply do better, whether job interviewing, dating, going to the doctor, buying a home, appreciating a work of art, or fending off criminals. And speaking of criminals, if for no other reason than to protect yourself from becoming a victim of crime, you'll want to pay attention to what follows in this book because criminals are *masters of observation*.

Catching Crooks

Frank Abagnale was one such criminal. In his autobiography, *Catch Me If You Can* (which was the basis for a 2002 film of the same name starring Leonardo DiCaprio), Mr. Abagnale exposes the many elaborate and intricate scams he masterminded. Once he posed as a commercial airline pilot and incredibly was given the controls of an in-flight passenger jetliner. In another caper, a hospital had hired him as a pediatrician that put emergency room patients in harm's way when he had to diagnose them. "What had made me [Mr. Abagnale recounted] so good as a con artist was my photographic memory ... And I was extremely *observant* [italics added], always noticing the small things that others didn't" (*Catch Me If You Can* 14).

Now back to the Pagoda – I guess I too had recognized way back in my teenage years that observing small things might serve a purpose, and that's why I counted those stairs (I still count). You see, our restaurant attracted its share of crooks too, diners who would literally eat and run – down those nineteen steps - without first paying the bill. All this despite our having a secret weapon - a little switch in the dining room that would activate a lock on the door at the bottom of the stairs. Sadly, we did not always reach that switch before the diner reached the door.

Therefore, we always had to judge if we were closer to the switch or closer to the stairs when a "crime" was in progress. The tipping point was to guess how far down those nineteen steps the fleeing diner had already descended to decide if it was more effective to give chase.

I must admit though that my record of "citizen arrests" pre-empted a career in law enforcement. On one occasion, we successfully made it to the switch in time only to witness the diner charging right *through* the locked plate glass door. Another time I gave chase after a much bigger fugitive down the stairs and out onto the street until I came to my senses – what would I do if I actually caught up to him, or worse, what would he do to me?

Questions. Period.

"Are there any questions?" Throughout my time in university (I had saved up enough money toiling at the restaurant to enrol), this call for questions marked the end of each class. If you glanced at my lecture notes and my textbooks, you would have seen underlining, highlighting, and arrows traversing pages like spaghetti. I wanted to learn so I usually had questions. But I seldom asked them when the lecturer made the call. Instead, the moment class ended I was up like a shot and made a dash for the front. Why? I wanted to ask my questions in private. It was the way I was raised – I think it's an Asian culture thing – you do not want to embarrass yourself by showing your weaknesses. Sadly, it's an impediment to learning.

If you too are hesitant to ask questions, there is hope. Every chapter in this book addresses this. It may take you some time, but over the years even I managed to shed my fear of asking questions. In 2008 I was at a forward-looking technology conference in San Francisco called *The Next Generation Data Center* (sounds more like a sci-fi film starring Leonard Nimoy). I had been invited to be a session panelist and also sat in on the keynote messages. In one such address, the speaker was Mark Sunday, then the Chief Information Officer of Oracle Corp., one of the world's largest software companies. After he concluded, he gave that familiar taunt: "Are there any questions?"

The room was packed with over one thousand attendees and there were microphones set up in the aisles. I rose without hesitation and proceeded to ask Mr. Sunday a very pointed question about whether Oracle actually used its own heavily marketed virtualization products to run its own business (he said "yes").

The point is, this time I did not flinch. If you have a question, you have to pursue the answer. But there's a right way to do this, so please read on.

Don't Just Take My Word For It

I have been following the career of the most famous National Hockey League (NHL) star, Sidney Crosby. Mr. Crosby (aka "The Kid") is the youngest team captain to win the NHL's championship, the Stanley Cup, and along the way he has snagged pretty much every other award available to him, from top scorer to Most Valuable Player ("Sidney Crosby").

That was all before Mr. Crosby was on the receiving end of a monstrous hit from David Steckel of the Washington Capitals in the NHL's 2011 outdoor winter classic that sidelined the star for almost a year with a serious concussion (Baker). This high profile injury triggered NHL rule changes, helmet manufacturer changes, and raised awareness in the media about concussions.

One such article noted: "'It takes an experienced professional about five minutes to assess whether a player likely suffered a concussion', he [Dr. Charles Tator, a University Health Network neurosurgeon] said. They have to be inquisitive and ferret out symptoms. You need to ask some *searching questions* [italics added] about how a player is functioning" (Duhatschek).

It's all about questions. The famous twentieth century Spanish painter, Pablo Picasso, had this insight attributed to him: "Computers are useless because they only give answers" ("Pablo Picasso Quotes"). In a forthcoming chapter, *Jump Start With Attributes*, you will find many searching questions on a broad spectrum of topics, including those related to concussion assessments.

In the 2011 superhero film, *Thor*, the title figure - the mythical god of thunder (played by Chris Hemsworth) - is cast down to earth by his father to learn a lesson on humility the hard way. Thor, newly exiled to planet earth, is still in shock, grappling with how far he has fallen figuratively and literally. Despite asking numerous questions of the earthlings (headlined by Natalie Portman) who first discover him, he remains confused about where he is. Finally Thor asks the senior scientist (portrayed by Stellan Skarsgard) why he cannot get any answers and the scientist replies that Thor is not asking the right questions. So with Hollywood thunder rumbling in the background, we have, courtesy of Thor, the key foundation for better observation:

Ask the right question, get the right answer.

Think about your own life and I believe you will agree with Thor:

- You are interviewed for a job but receive no offer. Most employers do not take the time to debrief unsuccessful applicants, but if you have (or make) the opportunity to ask, the most common question would go like this: "Why didn't I get the position?" – to which the most common answer would be: "You had good qualifications but someone else was better qualified".

  A better question would be "What do I need to improve to be successful in my next interview?" – this brings the focus directly to you and draws out invaluable insight. Asked properly, the right question might even lead you to another position with the company – good questions leave potential employers with a better impression of you.

- You go to your family doctor because you have trouble sleeping – a common affliction unfortunately. Suppose your doctor hands you a prescription for sleeping pills – also common and also unfortunate. Your first inclination might be to ask "Will I become dependent on these pills?" That's a fair question. But a better question would be "What can I do to uncover the *reason* for my sleep problem?"

  I can relate – once I too was offered the medication route but by asking the right question, I found myself at a sleep clinic instead. Since most sleep problems are diagnosed as sleep apnea (which is very treatable) you will be glad you asked the question too.

Full disclosure though – what you might not be so glad about is the actual sleep clinic experience. For me anyways it was a rude awakening (excuse the pun).

Arrival time at the clinic was late (11PM). First up, they shaved my legs and then taped every kind of electrode to me. Next, a tube was inserted in my nose. I climbed into a gurney-style bed and stared at a blinking overhead camera (looking now like Frankenstein). I couldn't move because of all the wires tethered to me. By this time it was past midnight, but I was informed I'd have to be up by 5:30AM. Following all of this turmoil I was ordered to sleep "normally" so I could be observed. There was nothing "normal" going on – I did not actually sleep at the "sleep clinic" at all!

What's The Problem?

Our ability to observe is directly related to our ability to ask good questions. Why do we not ask good questions anymore? I think our observing skills are in decline for these reasons:

- **No Reflection**: In a world of "instant" (think CNN, the Internet, social media, tweets, blogs), we can access a lot of information rapidly yet not think a whole lot about it all. Most school kids will tell you that something is true simply because they found it on Google. Content is king.

  But reflection requires time – we have to ponder, posit, and probe, and all that by asking good questions. But since we demand everything instantly, we either readily accept things or dismiss what is harder to accept by waving our hands and mumbling an apathetic "whatever".

- **No Curiosity**: Since we are overwhelmed by the flood of content from Google and Wikipedia, we become desensitized. To be curious about something, we have to zoom in and wonder out loud. Yet today, there's so much information, so much sensory overload (think *Harry Potter*) that we live our lives "zoomed out" and hence "tuned out". The result? *Everything* is declared "awesome" which in effect makes *nothing* awesome.

- **No Training**: While that overwhelming tsunami of content is in multi-media format, communication is still primarily through the medium of words. The person who can ask probing questions to "read between the lines" has the advantage in deciphering what the words are trying to convey. However, to analyze words, you must know something about grammar. This may bring back unpleasant grade school frustration, but grammar is a key to understanding communication. Since most people learn very little grammar anymore, our ability to observe will suffer (not to worry though, we will not be dwelling on grammar ahead).

We Will Learn From The Best

This general decline in observational skills is not to say that interest in questioning has declined. In fact, there are a number of question-oriented websites popping up like quora.com that try to connect one person's question with another person's answer, or Facebook Questions, which allows ad hoc polling on all manner of questions (like where's the best place to eat out).

Recently, (a very wealthy) someone paid USD$2.63 MM in a charity auction to win a lunch date with financial icon Warren Buffet, Chairman of Berkshire Hathaway (NYSE: BRK.A). Mr Buffet is one of the wealthiest men in the world (he has been donating his fortune to philanthropic causes through the foundation of another of the world's super rich – Bill Gates). I'm not sure where they had this expensive lunch or what was on the menu (chop suey?), but I would wager that the auction winner had prepared some good questions to ensure a decent return on the multi-million dollar investment.

So people are interested in questions – and good thing they are. Observation through good questioning is important for every pursuit in life. If you question this hypothesis, then you are proving the point! But you do not have to take my word for it – we're about to learn important principles in the pages that follow by gleaning from *the professionals who are paid to ask good questions.*

As a start, consider Larry King's succinct summary on asking good questions:

> "I'm in the Q&A Business. So I like questions. Not only do I like asking questions. I like answering them" (King 242).

Mr. King knows a thing or two about asking questions – he is an Emmy Award winning talk show host who until his recent retirement was the kingpin of TV news shows, anchoring *Larry King Live* for twenty-five years, and wearing his trademark suspenders for just about as long.

Maybe we will not all become suspender-wearing interviewers, but we can learn from Mr. King's attitude and techniques for asking questions. In fact in this book, we are going to turn to a number of experts who are in the "Q&A Business". Some of these elite question-askers are top media interviewers like Larry King, Mike Wallace, and David Frost, each of whom I'll introduce later with more biographical details. But beyond them, I asked myself "Who else is paid to ask good questions?" Doctors. Lawyers. Crime scene investigators. Police interrogators. There are many professionals who are paid to ask good questions, the right questions. We will learn from them all.

A Word About The Queen

Well, you already know that I will also be sharing with you the details of my quest for the Queen. As explained, I decided I would give myself a challenge to apply the observation lessons that I'll show you in the chapters to follow. My brain cramped trying to come up with the right person to pursue – someone world-famous, intriguing, and very difficult to access.

As I asked myself repeatedly the question "Who is the right person?" I pictured myself as Jack Ryan (played by Alec Baldwin) in the 1990 classic, *The Hunt For Red October*. In that film, Mr. Baldwin's character stands in the shower asking himself over and over how to entice Soviet sailors to abandon a nuclear submarine (the *Red October*) in the middle of the frigid north Atlantic. Not quite as famously as Jack Ryan, I too came to my own "aha moment" of clarity – I decided I would use the principles in this book to try to meet with Queen Elizabeth II, sovereign monarch of England since 1952 and the Head of fifteen Commonwealth nations (including Canada).

Well, you can't say I didn't aim high. And this choice certainly piqued my own curiosity. Would Her Majesty meet with me? Under what conditions? Would I have to wear a funny hat (they're called "fascinators" by the way, and thankfully, only women don them)?

Little did I realize at the time just how difficult it would be to meet the Queen. As I began my monarchy research, I learned first off that the Queen does not even grant media interviews so unless I became the head of state of some nation or gained international fame on screen or stage worthy of knighthood, I stood little chance, good questions or not, to meet the Queen. This would not be easy.

Throughout the pages to follow, I will chronicle how far I got (or how far away I remained) towards meeting the Queen, using only the principles described herein. So as I imagine you might hear the Queen herself announce in full rarefied British accent, shall we begin?

Presenting Her Majesty Queen Elizabeth II

Just in case you have not met the Queen lately, here are a few quick facts:

- Born: April 21, 1926
- Eldest daughter of King George VI and Queen Elizabeth (the Queen Mother)
- Married Prince Philip November 20, 1947
- Children: Prince Charles, Princess Anne, Prince Andrew, Prince Edward
- Ascension: February 6, 1952 after the death of her father

- The Queen is Head of State of the United Kingdom and fifteen Commonwealth nations.
- As Head of State, the Queen is responsible for "constitutional acts, including the opening of Parliament, the approval of Orders in Council, signing of Acts of Parliament and weekly meetings with the Prime Minister."

- "The Queen represents Britain on overseas State visits as well as receiving foreign ambassadors, high commissioners and visiting Heads of State."
- "As Head of the Nation, Queen Elizabeth II represents the national identity, unity and pride of Britain."

("The Role of the Sovereign")

Chapter 2

THE SECRET SAUCE

The Positive Side

Well, you now know that I grew up in a restaurant family, so the "secret sauce" metaphor has extra meaning! As you can imagine, we had many secret sauces – pineapple, honey garlic, sweet and sour to name a few. I especially enjoyed our plum sauce – not the kind in those little tear-open packets that come with take-out food, but the kind we served our diners in porcelain saucers alongside egg rolls. One day I observed one of my uncles making the plum sauce in the kitchen and if you contact me with a good question I'll let you in on the secret ingredient!

Right now, I will let you in on my "secret sauce" (actually sauces) for asking good questions – these principles came from my research into how the "Q&A experts" ply their trade. Here are the so-called "APT™ Principles", divided into three segments:

FIGURE 2-1 The APT Principles

A **ATTITUDE**	Be Curious Be Creative Be Persistent Be Thorough Be Skeptical
P **PREPARATION**	Have A Specific Objective Do Your Homework Know Your Audience Choose The Right Person Don't Assume
T **TECHNIQUE**	Watch Your Language Listen Actively Soften Up Your Audience Ask Short Simple Questions Look for Inconsistencies

The first thing to note is that there are *fifteen* principles. Now, you may find certain principles more your style than others. You might find only a subset of the principles useful to you. You might apply the principles in a seemingly random order.

While there is a certain logic here - you really should first develop the right Attitudes (segment one) which then lead into proper Preparation (segment two) that finally powers effective Techniques (segment three) - the principles in the three segments are all inter-related and inter-dependent, and need not be applied in any rigid sequence.

The attitudes in fact permeate *every* segment – for example, if you are creative (the Attitude segment), then that "outside-the-box" thinking will be reflected in how you do your homework (the

Preparation segment) which will influence how you soften up your audience (the Technique segment) in a uniquely creative way.

As another example, suppose you aim to choose the right person to ask a question of (the Preparation segment). You will most likely work through multiple people, perhaps by asking short simple questions (the Technique segment) to each person in succession until you finally settle on that right person to ask the questions that will satisfy your specific objective (the Preparation segment).

The Negative Side

Note also that the last principle in each segment has a negative connotation. These negatives allow you to "check your work" like your math teacher always used to say. For example, in the Attitude segment, as you work on becoming curious, creative, persistent, and thorough, you must also add a dollop of *skepticism* – a reality check - to ensure that your observations are valid.

In the Preparation segment, review all your preparation work by sussing out any *assumptions* that may be lurking behind your questions. Finally, in the Technique segment, you must constantly be vigilant to sniff out *inconsistencies* – things that do not add up – in what you are observing, as these seemingly minor details often lead to breakthroughs.

FIGURE 2-2 The "Negative" APT Principles

A ATTITUDE	Be Curious Be Creative Be Persistent Be Thorough **Be Skeptical** ←
P PREPARATION	Have A Specific Objective Do Your Homework Know Your Audience Choose The Right Person **Don't Assume** ←
T TECHNIQUE	Watch Your Language Listen Actively Soften Up Your Audience Ask Short Simple Questions **Look for Inconsistencies** ←

APT Segment One: Attitude

Attitude is where it all begins. Earlier I lamented that curiosity (one of the Attitudes) is in decline. Is it a "nature vs. nurture" thing? I believe some people are born with more curiosity than others but everyone can learn to develop curiosity (as well as the other attitudes in the segment).

Consider senior citizens. Lifespans are increasing due to better living standards, so the pool of seniors is much deeper than even a generation ago. I doubt that every senior started out in childhood as the most observant person, but if you want to know what's going on, say in your neighbourhood, ask a senior. Not much escapes a senior's notice.

Right now as I write I am having a roof repair done but the voices I hear outside are not the contractors hammering down shingles, but two of my curious older neighbours stopping by to quiz the hired help on what they are doing. I count on my "greying friends" to set me straight on what the garbage collector is collecting this week and to report whether there have been any suspicious people loitering in my backyard (there have been, but the seniors reportedly scared them off!).

Seniors just seem to observe more – sure they have more time on their hands to watch everything going on in the neighbourhood - but they also have learned to use this time to advantage. Bottom line – there is hope for you to learn to be more curious (and more creative, persistent, thorough, and skeptical) ... and you do not need to wait till retirement.

APT Segment Two: Preparation

Attitude is number one, but without preparation, not much will result. Attitude without preparation is as futile as desire without diligence – sort of like wanting to lose weight but not having the strength to start exercising. Observation and questioning take preparation and lots of hard work to get going.

The principles in the Preparation segment of knowing your audience and of doing your homework came primarily out of the context of media interviewers like Barbara Walters who committed to significant background research on each of her guests before conducting an interview. To go in unprepared would have been very cavalier for Ms. Walters, who prides herself on being thoroughly immersed in her subject before engaging in a one-on-one talk.

On the other hand, some vocations demand results with very little, if any prior preparation – sales can be like that. If you've ever been handed a phone book or a call sheet and told to "cold call" total strangers out-of-the-blue, what does preparation mean then? I wear many hats, one being a business strategy consultant. I am sometimes requested to help clients develop a sales and marketing strategy, and this often includes coaching sales people so that they can execute the strategy.

I would train sales teams to recognize the importance of every shred of information about a customer but also to realize that all information has a "shelf life". In sales, preparation begins with a careful review of every piece of information gleaned from a prospect for leveraging later. A sales person who reports to management that a prospect is not interested in a product has to keep digging by asking good questions until the real reason for disinterest is surfaced. On many occasions I have been told that a prospect had no interest in speaking with my client only to learn by calling that prospect myself that the prospect is actually willing to book a follow-up meeting. Ask the right question, get the right answer.

In terms of preparation, it's all about not giving up, about digging in, building to a plan of attack one detail at a time. Later you will encounter stories of patients saved from life-threatening disease and perjurers exposed in court precisely because the doctor or lawyer paid attention to details and built the right conclusion from them.

APT Segment Three: Technique

Finally we come to technique. I am frequently told that people learn in different ways – some are "kinesthetic learners", meaning they have to learn by doing things hands-on, others are "visual learners" who learn best by watching others, while still others are "auditory learners" who learn best by listening or reading out loud (EduGuide Staff). What all this means for us is that you may find some of the techniques more consistent with your learning style than others, but I encourage you to learn all of the techniques.

Of the different techniques, I have found that the starting point is always to "Have a Specific Objective", as this serves to anchor everything else. If you are clear as to what you are aiming to learn in your observation, then with the right attitude and preparation, you will be more successful.

Now that we have completed our jiffy overview of the three segments of the APT Principles, I hope you are curious to learn more because we will now examine each principle in turn.

Chapter 3

ATTITUDE – BE CURIOUS

By George, Notice Anything Curious?

Do you play cards? You know, hearts, Texas Hold 'Em, rummy, bridge, crazy eights, president, even solitaire? Have you ever noticed anything unusual about any of the cards, say the jacks in the deck? Picture them now – the easy part is to recognize that there are of course four jacks, one for each suit – spades, clubs, hearts, diamonds. But what else do you recall?

Not long ago, it was pointed out to me that some jacks are "one-eyed". You see, the Jack of Hearts, (as well as the Jack of Spades and the King of Diamonds) are drawn in side profile (these cards are commonly called "one-eyed"), while the rest of the courts (or face cards) are shown in full face (i.e. with two eyes showing) ("Standard 52-card Deck"). Do you know why?

Compare for example these two Jacks to see the differences (besides the suit):

FIGURE 3-1 Two Different Jacks

Source: Copyright Christos Georghiou /Shutterstock.com. Used by permission.

I never noticed these differences before. According to Wikipedia, the playing cards we typically use today are of French origin. The United States Playing Card Company (they make the well-known "Bicycle" brand of cards) suggests that various cards represented *different figures* in history (e.g. the King of Hearts was Charlemagne of France, the King of Diamonds was Julius Caesar, the King of Clubs was Alexander the Great, and the King of Spades was King David of the Bible) ("52-Card Deck").

I guess I failed to show curiosity with playing cards because I was concentrating more on trying to win whatever game I was playing! However, curiosity is a must-have attitude to become a good observer.

When Steve Jobs had a falling out with then-Disney CEO Michael Eisner, Mr. Jobs derided Mr. Eisner by chiding "He [Mr. Eisner] was never curious. I [Mr. Jobs] was amazed. Curiosity is very important" (Isaacson 433).

Curious people look harder, dig deeper, and think longer about what they observe, which causes them to come away with better, more enduring observations. Take a look at the Discovery Channel's website curiosity.com if you want to stretch your curiosity.

Here are two more examples of curiosity, one ridiculous, one more sublime:

- If you watch any professional team sports like hockey, football, or basketball at playoff time, you always see the championship team donning caps and t-shirts proclaiming their #1 status (e.g. "2012 World Series Champions" etc.) the very moment the game ends. I always wanted to ask what happens to all those t-shirts and hats that were made for the team that *did not* win. These would become immediate collectors' items, sort of like coins or postage stamps produced with imperfections.

- Now for the sublime. Have you ever wondered how the Great Pyramid at Giza (Egypt) was constructed? There were no cranes, no forklift trucks, no dump trucks – sure slave labour was plentiful back around 2551 BC when the Egyptian Pharaoh Khufu began his rule by building his burial tomb - but the Great Pyramid measures about 758 feet (231 m) on each side of the base and is constructed of limestone blocks, each block weighing about 2.5 tons (2.3 metric tons).

So how did the workers lift these blocks to build the walls? Some archaeologists theorize that "workers built dirt ramps along the sides of the pyramid. Workers rolled blocks up the ramp and into position on the pyramid wall. When they were ready to begin the next layer, workers added more dirt to the ramp to make it higher. After the pyramid was finished, workers removed the dirt ramp with shovels. Other archaeologists, however, say that it would have been too difficult to build and use the ramps" (Woods, and Woods 8-12).

A more intriguing hypothesis is that the Egyptians learned how to reduce limestone blocks into *powder*, and then poured that powder into molds *in place*, adding water, lime, and natron (sodium carbonate). Once left to dry in the sun, the blocks would be formed exactly where they were placed. Now that's a much better idea (if true) which satisfies curiosity and increases admiration for the engineering prowess of the Egyptians (Dumont-Le Cornec 23).

From Leonardo to Larry

Whom do you know that is curious? We can learn from watching others in their natural habitat, especially when that habitat is television. You can take your pick of famous TV interviewers who are annually paid millions of dollars to ask the kinds of questions that often make their guests pause, or cringe - which usually means something is about to be disclosed that just might be off-script. Love him or hate him (suspenders and gaudy ties included), Larry King is one such expert interviewer.

"Naturally I loved to ask those [deeper] questions if I had the time; that was the pleasure of that Sunday night show in Miami; I could go as far as my **curiosity** [bold face and underscoring added] would take me" (King 71).

Later in his career, Mr. King would let us in on his secret for interviewing US presidents: "I look at the president with the same curiosity I have for the plumber. I think that's what separated me from everyone else in the business" (218). And speaking of presidents, Mr. King observed the following about President George W. Bush "[Mr. Bush's] problem was that he has no curiosity. He doesn't wonder about things. That's a major failing" (232).

In his book, *How To Think Like Leonardo da Vinci*, Michael Gelb has studied the life and sometimes peculiar practices of the famous artist (and inventor and scientist) to extract seven principles that would presumably help us to move closer to genius-hood. The very first secret on the list? Curiosity (or "Curiosita" in Italian).

Mr. Gelb defines "curiosita" as "an insatiably curious approach to life and an unrelenting quest for continuous learning" (48). Let's forget for the moment that this definition is "circular", i.e. that "curious" is used to help define what it means to be curious! The big adverbs and adjectives - insatiably, unrelenting, continuous - all point to an attitude of persistent probing. Mr. Gelb presents considerable evidence that Leonardo da Vinci had curiosity in abundance:

- Leonardo the inventor had made plans for a helicopter, parachute, extendable ladder, bicycle, three gear speed shifter, adjustable wrench, hydraulic jack, canal locks, folding furniture, a snorkel, and a water powered alarm clock, to name but a few of his sketched inventions (43).

- Leonardo the engineer had considered designs for tanks, mortars, missiles, even submarines (43).

- Leonardo the scientist anticipated breakthroughs by Newton (gravity), Copernicus (the earth revolves around the sun), and Galileo (the telescope) (45).

Cultivating Curiosity

This great curiosity is attributed by Mr. Gelb in part to the ability to ask penetrating questions. "As soon as they can speak, children start articulating question after question" (49). Later he states that "Great minds go on asking confounding questions with the same intensity throughout their lives" (49).

Leonardo would ask questions like "Why shells existed on the tops of mountains along with the imprints of coral and plants and seaweed usually found in the sea; why the thunder lasts a longer time than that which causes it …" (Gelb 50).

Mr. Gelb goes on to suggest ways that we can develop curiosity, "by cultivating a Da Vinci-like open, questing frame of mind …" (55). The first approach is simply to carry a notebook around (or these days, your favourite electronic gadget for taking notes). Apparently, Leonardo was constantly jotting down his observations and questions. I can tell you that this simple first step works. Having been the CEO of more than one software startup, I always observed who would bring a notebook or pad of paper into meetings – anyone who wasn't so equipped was in my "bad books" because it signalled to me that there was no serious intention to take action based on whatever would come out of the discussion.

It's kind of like that saying – if you pray for rain and do not carry an umbrella you really do not think anything is going to happen. Since I do not have the greatest memory, I have a double incentive to document diligently. I am always taking notes so that I do not forget my observations, whether it is the library call number on a book on sailing, or the name of a good plumber that a friend recommends.

Once you've built up the habit of carrying a notebook around so that you are always poised to record, you need to hone your content.

Not surprisingly, the quality of what you write down is improved by learning how to ask good questions. Mr. Gelb points out and I heartily agree that this can be a challenge to us because our school systems train students to give the right *answer* rather than asking the right question. Now, content is important, but without curiosity, the student may not have learned a thing, except how to regurgitate the answer.

I once received 99% on a fourth year university math final exam because I just happened to study all the proofs and derivations that ended up being on the test – so I could give the precise answers the instructor sought. I doubt that I could explain any of the content now (the course was "differential geometry" – do not even ask what that means!). Too often teachers are annoyed with students who ask too many questions – yet the old adage that "there are no dumb questions" still holds true.

In order to develop curiosity through question-asking skills, Mr. Gelb points out that Leonardo often began with simple, even naïve questions like "Why is the sky blue?" Practising using the "W5+H" method of formulating "Who, What, Where, When, Why, How" questions is a natural progression from there. I often teach primary school-aged children in my church and I drill them on "W5+H" – I might bring in an unusual household object and keep it hidden. One student will remain out of view and take a look at the object, while the other students are tasked with asking that volunteer "W5+H" questions to try to guess the object. These questioners then draw what they think their questions have uncovered. Sometimes the results are close, but often they are way off! But week-by-week, they improve, and so can we.

30   How To Meet The Queen

Let's try an example right now. Look at the picture below and come up with at least one question in each of the six "W5+H" categories:

FIGURE 3-2 "Mystery Object"

Source: Copyright 1999-2012 DV724. Used by Permission.

Put your questions here or jot them down in your notebook:

TABLE 3-1 W5+H Questions

WHO	
WHAT	
WHERE	
WHEN	
WHY	
HOW	

Just so you have an idea of how this might all look, here are some questions I came up with:

TABLE 3-2 W5+H Questions: Suggestions

WHO	Who would use this thing?
	Who made this?
	Who does this belong to?
	Who is going to tell me what it is?
WHAT	What is this used for?
	What is it made of?
	What parts move?
	What sizes does it come in?
	What is the point of this exercise?
WHERE	Where is this made?
	Where is this sold?
WHEN	When was this manufactured?
	When is it used?
	When was this first invented?
WHY	Why does it have a knurled shaft?
	Why is one end smaller than the other?
HOW	How much does it cost?
	How does it work?
	How big is it?

Another question: how did you feel doing this exercise? It should have caused you to knit your eyebrows together as you concentrated and stared at this foreign object. Some "W5+H" categories (like "What") might have been easier for you to come up with questions and some categories might have been more challenging (like "When"). This is typical. You might feel like a headache is coming on! This may be typical too, at least for the beginning observer, but once you start to exercise with your notepad and questions, your curiosity will improve as will your ability to ask more incisive questions.

Of course, some people will have advantages over others in asking good questions depending on the subject – we will cover this more in the chapter *Jump Start With Attributes*. And before I forget, you probably would like to know what that "mystery object" really is … it's a little hand-sized guitar stringing widget. If you play guitar, you know it takes time to put new strings on, with the most labour required to turn the tuning pegs (I used to have a twelve string guitar – twice the fun) so that the guitar string wraps many times around the tuning post (otherwise the string will slip and go out of tune easily). The mystery widget allows you to rapidly turn the tuning pegs with minimal effort.

Curiosity And The Queen

As promised, I want to chronicle my quest to try to meet with Her Majesty, Queen Elizabeth II, and so here I need to connect up the first stop in the APT Principles, curiosity, with that quest.

It was April 2011 and I was standing in the basement of my church after an Easter Good Friday service. There we were clutching hot cross buns engaged in small pockets of conversation. In front of me was someone I'd met only that day. He was evasive when I began my litany of questions – done in good taste I hope – but a litany nonetheless. When I got to asking him his occupation he told me he was a stand-up comic. My *curiosity* was piqued. So naturally I asked him about his material and he immediately proceeded to share some of his risqué material on me – blush, blush – I had to remind him we were standing in a church!

I figure that most comedians are intelligent and observant people who also excel at public speaking so I next asked this newcomer if he had honed his comedic craft in school. I went further, to venture that he must have attended the toniest school in town, that being Upper Canada College (one of Canada's elite schools, founded in 1829, which produced many famous alumni including twenty-four Rhodes Scholars) ("Upper Canada College").

That led to his disclosure that he hadn't attended school nearby, he had gone to a private school in the city of Peterborough (about two hours east of Toronto). Never to let "sleeping dogs" lie, I asked him for the name of the school – it was Lakefield College – the same school that Prince Andrew had attended (that would be His Royal Highness, Prince Andrew, Duke of York, second son of Her Majesty Queen Elizabeth II, and former husband of Sarah Ferguson, aka "Fergie").

Wow. Of course, then he shared his personal opinions of the Prince and we were done eating the hot cross buns. The conversation ended, but it took a serendipitous course down a path of great interest to me – a royal path – all as a result of curiosity.

Moments later I was having lunch with friends whereupon I regaled them with my tale about Prince Andrew when just then a friend at the table offered up *another* connection to the Royal Family ... my quest was off to a good start.

Chapter 4

ATTITUDE – BE CREATIVE

Making Something Out Of Nothing

If curiosity is the attitude of wanting to go deeper to explore something, creativity is the attitude of going wider, making something new that goes beyond typical boundaries. Think of someone you know who is creative – maybe you came up with someone "artsy", who is good at some area of arts and crafts. My wife is a nursery school teacher so I've had the opportunity to observe every manner of innovation involving toilet paper rolls (every teacher's favourite craft material) to clothes hangers (for creating mobiles) to pop bottles (for demonstrating mini-tornadoes). Not that creativity is limited to arts. Some are creative with words (think poetry, or advertising copy), some with sounds (music), some with foods (famous chefs cannot make any dish look ordinary) ... you get the picture.

Robert Dennard is the renowned IBM researcher responsible for inventing dynamic random access memory – the foundation for the memory in your laptop, tablet, smartphone, you name it ("Robert H. Dennard"). Mr. Dennard defines creativity in "The Innovator's

Toolkit" from Harvard Business School Publishing as "the ability to produce or bring into existence something that was not there before, something new, an extension of our base of knowledge" (167).

When we think about creativity, we expect teachers and researchers (and musicians, and artists, and ...) to be creative in their professions. But some vocations seem to eschew creativity. There is the common tongue-in-cheek reference to "creative accountants" (implying that such accountants are manipulating the books). How about medicine? Would you like a "creative doctor"?

Probably not, if that means that the doctor is making up treatments or abandoning the rigours of medical science in exchange for free expression. However, Dr. Jerome Groopman has a different opinion on creativity.

Dr. Groopman is the Chair of Medicine at Harvard Medical School, the Chief of Experimental Medicine at Beth Israel Deaconess Medical Center (Boston), and interestingly, a Staff Writer at The New Yorker. Pretty solid credentials if you ask me. He wrote some extraordinary books for physicians to exhort them to re-think how they practice medicine. In one of his books, *How Doctors Think*, Dr. Groopman warns that "Clinical algorithms can be useful for run-of-the-mill diagnosis and treatment ... But they quickly fall apart when a doctor needs to think outside their boxes ... algorithms discourage physicians from thinking independently and *creatively* [italics added]" (5).

We will encounter Dr. Groopman again in the following chapters. He will recount real-life patient case histories where a lack of proper questioning contributed to avoidable complications and suffering – these cautionary tales should motivate you to learn everything you can about asking better questions.

When I was in high school, we ran an annual career fair called "Symposium" that let students select careers of interest and then receive a computer-generated schedule of which talks they could attend to hear experts expound on different careers (I once took a survey that told me I should be a bus driver – I sure messed that one up).

The problem with this whole selection process lay with how computing was done in those early days of technology. When I was in high school, computer programs were transcribed line-by-line onto punch cards (you probably have no idea what I'm talking about) that were submitted to a central school board computer once a week to be executed, with the resulting printouts sent back to each school many days later. There was no PC, no iPhone, no cell phones at all, no Internet - just a few big computers locked away that executed programs that lived on cardboard punch cards.

Well, to make matters worse, we missed the weekly cut-off to submit the computer program that was intended to sort through everyone's choices for the Symposium. The student leader responsible for the career fair was in tears and the teachers and students responsible for the programming were debating with each other. I walked into this chaos and immediately turned around and headed to the Principal's office (no, I wasn't sent there). I took a phone directory and called the community college in our city, figuring that they had a computer we might be able to use. I asked to be connected to someone in the computer centre, described our problem, was asked who our teacher was, found out that the computer operator knew our teacher, and soon enough we got our program run. You may tire of hearing me repeat in this book a simple axiom:

Ask the right question, get the right answer.

In this case, I was able to *create* a new solution that everyone else had overlooked – the student programmers and the teacher supervisors had constrained themselves to only one solution – the school board computer. But once we could remove that constraint and think *beyond* that boundary, a new solution could be found. The creative question that I had asked myself was "If the school board couldn't help us, who else had a big enough computer that might help us out?"

Creative people look at the same things everyone else looks at but see something different – a twist, a possibility, an opening. If you go to an art gallery you'll see lots of seemingly "twisted" exhibits! Recently I was at the local gallery where there was an exhibit that conveyed what I'd have to say is a shoe fetish – the artist had shoes prominently in his work in the most bizarre (aka creative) scenarios. For example, in one vignette, a bartender was pouring a drink into a woman's high heeled shoe that was positioned over the head of a patron lying on his back – there was a hole in the heel that allowed a stream to make its way down to his face. I don't think I have space on my living room wall for that one.

Take The Test

Now I'm not singling out artists, but this gallery experience made me think about doing a little search for creativity tools, which led me to the Art Institute of Vancouver. If you visit their website, you'll find a "Right Brain vs. Left Brain Creativity Test" – I guess if you score as highly creative (I did not, being an avowed lefty head), you would then go on to apply to the Institute to study there – interesting recruiting tool.

So if you are so-inclined (if you are time conscious or too structured like me then it's already game-over) the link is:

> http://www.wherecreativitygoestoschool.com/vancouver/left_right/rb_test.htm

Here is a sample of the types of questions you'll be asked ("Right Brain vs. Left Brain Creativity Test"):

- "I need complete quietness to study."

- "I prefer to be in a group."

- "I have the ability to listen to music or television and study at the same time."

- "I prefer to have visual instructions with examples."

- "When I set goals for myself, it helps me to keep from procrastinating."

It's fairly obvious that you can tilt the results by guessing how to answer each question so that you can be branded as either a left-brained or right-brained person, particularly when some of the less subtle questions are:

- "I enjoy doing or learning math."

- "I enjoy doing or learning algebra."

- "I have thought about becoming a lawyer, librarian, mathematician, lab scientist, or doctor."

What is it about us mathematicians that make them the left brain poster child?

Seeing Outside The Box

Come to think of it, I should expand my working definition of creativity. Not only do creative people look at the same things everyone else looks at but see something different, they also do the opposite – creative people do *not* see the constraints or limitations that everyone else can see. Put it this way: we always talk about "seeing outside the box" … well, creative people sometimes do not see any box at all!

There are many famous accounts of inventions that came from creative minds that saw what others could not see (or did not see the obstacles that others saw). 3M's famous Post-It Notes (aka Sticky Notes) is a case in point – the manufacturer had produced a new glue that failed to be sticky enough to work as planned. Most would have chalked this up as a failure and written it off, as is more often than not the fate of research and development work. However, some bright (creative) person recognized the market potential for a low grade adhesive and Post-It Notes were born ("Post-It Notes").

Another example: I received a flyer the other day from PuroClean, a mould removal company, which touted itself as "The Paramedics of Property Damage". The combination of two or more things that do not normally belong together points to creativity. This "mash up" of concepts is also advocated by the medical profession, which encourages practitioners to try to think outside the box by correlating seemingly contradictory diagnostic evidence that doesn't usually belong together.

In "The Innovator's Toolkit", creativity is enhanced by "… fresh perspectives that are unencumbered by the prevailing wisdom or established ways of doing things. Often called a 'beginner's mind', this is the perspective of a newcomer: a person who is curious, even playful, and willing to ask anything – no matter how naïve the question may seem – because she doesn't know what she doesn't know. Thus, bringing together contradictory characteristics can catalyze new ideas." (177).

Doing The "Out-Of-The-Box" Step

Now, to confound the left vs. right brain adherents, let me suggest a left brain process that may help you improve your right brain creativity for any given situation:

- Ask yourself what the ultimate objective is

- Identify all the constraints, and

- Ask additional questions to try to address the objective by removing one constraint at a time

Let's try this out:

TABLE 4-1 Identifying and Removing Constraints (Swim Lesson Scenario)

Situation	Objective	Constraints	Removing Constraints
You are driving a child to a swim class but you are going to be late.	Learn how to do the front crawl. (You might have thought the objective was to reach class on time, but that's not the real objective).	Traffic will not allow you to go faster.	Remove the speed limit and go faster (that could score you a nice speeding ticket!).
		Class starts at a fixed time.	When you arrive, ask if you can stay late to make-up for what you missed.
		The number of classes is fixed.	Ask if you can book an extra lesson – even a private lesson – so that the front crawl can be learned.

Maybe that test scenario seems too trivial but creativity really does drive better questioning, and that can lead to unexpected results. Consider this example from World War II. Before the US entered the War, the UK was under constant bombardment and imminent invasion in its war with Germany. In a desperate letter dated December 8, 1940, the UK Prime Minister, Winston Churchill, appealed convincingly to the US President, Franklin D. Roosevelt for material and supplies, employing typically eloquent but forceful language like this:

Attitude – Be Creative   43

The moment approaches when we shall no longer be able to pay cash for shipping and other supplies. While we will do our utmost, and shrink from no proper sacrifice to make payments across the Exchange, I believe you will agree that it would be wrong in principle and mutually disadvantageous in effect, if at the height of this struggle, Great Britain were to be divested of all salable assets, so that after the victory was won with our blood, civilisation saved, and the time gained for the United States to be fully armed against all eventualities, we should stand stripped to the bone. Such a course would not be in the moral or the economic interests of either of our countries ("Churchill Seeks Support From Roosevelt").

Mr. Roosevelt wrestled with this almost impossible situation. Up to the time of Mr. Churchill's letter, the US had passed the Johnson Act of 1934, which forbade the US from extending credit terms to any of its allies that had defaulted on loans in World War I – and the UK was among the defaulters. Subsequent legislation in the Neutrality Act of 1939 went further - the US could only sell military supplies to nations on a cash basis.

However, the UK was cash-strapped and simply could not afford to pay for supplies. So what to do? The UK was on the verge of collapse, London was being turned into rubble, Germany was amassing an invasion force across the English Channel. Meanwhile, Mr. Roosevelt's own senior military advisers were vehemently opposed to providing tanks, ships, and other material to the UK for fear that if the UK succumbed, these would all fall into enemy hands.

Instead of admitting defeat, Mr. Roosevelt asked himself a *creative* question: how could he give the UK the material it required to fight Hitler without cost? Here's the summary of the situation:

TABLE 4-2 Identifying and Removing Constraints (World War II)

Situation	Objective	Constraints	Removing Constraints
The UK faced defeat to Germany without more military supplies.	Provide the UK with the needed supplies.	The UK had no cash to pay.	(see below)
		The US could not extend credit terms.	
		The US military opposed sending supplies that could be taken by Germany.	

Mr. Roosevelt's creative solution was twofold: the "Destroyers for Bases" Agreement and the Lend-Lease Act.

"Destroyers for Bases" allowed the US to give, free of charge, fifty old destroyers to the UK in exchange for access to some British naval bases. This removed the constraint put up by the US military brass, since this gave the US strategic military advantages.

The Lend-Lease Act removed the constraint of cost recovery for other material. In exchange for supplies at no cost, the UK agreed to co-operate with the US to create a new economic order following the

War. Mr. Roosevelt famously likened it to lending a garden hose to a neighbour whose house is on fire — the lender wouldn't ask for repayment, just for return of the hose after the fire was put out, which by the way would then prevent the fire from spreading to the lender's home ("Milestones: 1937-1945").

While many in the US were opposed to these agreements, they arguably set the stage for a change in the War's outcome. The US President asked the right question and was able to craft a political and military solution that removed the constraints that shackled everyone else.

The Job Of Creativity

Job interviews are front-line opportunities for creative questioning. I'll be using some examples from interviewing in the chapter, *Attitude - Be Skeptical*. For now, let me say that I've heard all the textbook kinds of questions and responses in interviews. In contrast, here are a few questions that are more creative:

- At the end of an interview, an interviewer might ask "What questions should I have been asking you that I missed?" - this lets the candidate bring out other qualities or anecdotes that standard questioning failed to draw out, and also allows a candidate to make a summary case for why the candidate should be hired.

- Some interviewers like to ask unexpected questions like "What was the last non-work related book you read and what did you think about it?" This allows the interviewer to observe whether a candidate can think on-the-fly and also can expose how the candidate likes to learn (it is commonly said that "readers are leaders" – depending of course on what is being read).

- Another creative interview question that I know is used on occasion is "If you could be any kitchen implement (like a vegetable peeler or a measuring spoon), which would you be and why?" This question can fluster candidates but this question goes outside the box to uncover how much reflection a candidate does (in the chapter *Jump Start With Attributes*, this quality of reflection is sought after by top interviewers as a differentiator in high quality candidates). You should pause right now and prove to yourself that you can reflect by deciding if you are a flour sifter or a garlic press!

The Power Of Creativity

In *How To Interview – The Art of the Media Interview*, author Paul McLaughlin recounts an interview that radio broadcaster Stuart McLean conducted with Hollywood actor Jack Lemmon, Academy Award winner and star of over sixty movies in the late twentieth century. Mr. Lemmon's handler arranged for each media interviewer to have only fifteen minutes to ask questions (161).

Mr. McLean decided he had to take a creative approach to have a better interview. He spent three days researching and watching Mr. Lemmon's films. He compiled many obscure facts about Mr. Lemmon and then during the fifteen minute interview, asked if Mr. Lemmon would like to play a word association game. In the game, Mr. McLean used these facts, and soon Mr. Lemmon was warm to the interviewer, which resulted in a lively, interesting interview with many personal anecdotes.

In my own experience in the software business I learned firsthand the power of creative questions. Around the year 2003 I was looking for new ideas for a software startup. The notorious "dot-com" days were long gone when business plans written literally on the back of a napkin were getting millions in funding from big name venture capital (VC) firms.

I took one idea to a VC that had recently backed a Canadian startup that was acquired by IBM for several million dollars - initially the VC liked the pitch. But after about four to five months of meetings and optimism I was told the idea, though still valid, was late to market.

If you've ever been involved in a startup in any industry, you know that getting your hopes up and your "bubble burst" is common, and that more than ninety percent of startups crash and burn. This failure was just another statistic – but I needed to learn from this rejection.

I kept asking myself what turned out to be the pivotal creative questions:

- "How can a small company with no budget afford to do leading-edge research to come up with innovative ideas?"

- "How can a small company ever develop a ground-breaking idea ahead of the competition that will not be late to market?"

- "Who is paid to do advanced research that we might leverage as our own research and development arm?"

Aha! (that's the clichéd "aha" or "eureka" moment that entrepreneurs like to shriek). The questioning process allowed me to identify the objective, the constraints, and then get outside the box to a creative solution: go talk to academics. University researchers are paid to churn out leading-edge academic papers ("publish or perish") though these luminaries often have little interest (or awareness) of commercialization value.

Our senior management team already had a clear sense of what technology we wanted to build, so once we started to navigate through academia, we were able to find newly published research that would lead us to our own patentable software product. Within five years of closing our first round of VC funding, our company was acquired by a big public technology company and we were able to join the ranks of successful entrepreneurs. So do not tell me that good questions do not pay off!

Here for completeness is the chart for the startup scenario:

TABLE 4-3 Identifying and Removing Constraints (Startups)

Situation	Objective	Constraints	Removing Constraints
Create a new startup to generate new intellectual property leading to financial upside.	Identify a new idea to develop and bring to market.	Budget is too small to create new technology.	Reach out to academics who have budgets and staff to do advanced research, but who have low interest in commercializing research.
		New ideas take too long to bring to market ahead of competition.	

By this point you should understand that regardless of your natural creativity, it is possible for you to improve creativity by sizing up the situation, zeroing in on the objective, identifying the constraints (the box) and to ask creative questions to take you beyond the box and on the way to meeting the objective.

Creativity and the Queen

So now let's continue our saga of the quest to meet the Queen.

From the previous chapter I left off having found a person who had been school-mates with the Queen's son, Prince Andrew, as a result of asking questions prompted by curiosity. It wasn't even thirty minutes after I met this total stranger that I was having lunch with some friends. Naturally, I retold the story of this connection with Her Majesty when wouldn't you know it – the degrees of separation between me and the Queen fell another notch.

It turns out that a friend of mine had been a foreign student in London after World War II studying to be a nurse. The then recently crowned Queen would hold garden parties from time-to-time at Buckingham Palace and on occasion invited foreign students among the other guests. My heart raced as I blurted out the obvious next questions …

- "Did she [my friend] meet the Queen personally?"
  (no, she almost did, but then a friend of hers was selected to have that honour).

- "Did she keep a copy of the invitation?"
  (no, poor students in those days did not have the luxury of storage space to keep many personal items).

My hopes of somehow picking up the trail were dashed but I maintained a persistent attitude (more on that in the chapter to come) – having survived in a software startup builds a lot of character!

Later I would do some intensive background research on Her Majesty (covered in the chapter *Preparation – Know Your Audience*), but still the challenge remained: how would I, who had no direct connection with the Queen, *create* a means to meet with her?

I mean, thousands have met with the Queen over her long reign (sixty years in 2012) and thousands more would like to have that chance. Why would I be able to advance in this queue of royal watchers? I began to ask myself that question more specifically … "What connection could I create with the Queen that might increase my odds of meeting her one day?" It seemed like a classic "chicken and egg" conundrum – to meet the Queen you need to have a connection, but to have a connection, you need to have already met the Queen.

As these constraints, this box that fenced in my objective of meeting the Queen, played out in my mind, the answer to the question suggested a creative solution: I would *make my own connection* first. No, I wasn't planning to scale the Palace walls and rappel myself in. The creative idea was to leverage the concepts of the social networking website, LinkedIn.com.

Being an entrepreneur, I have much admiration for LinkedIn. If you've never visited this site, it is like Facebook for professionals, based on the "six degrees of separation" concept, i.e. if two people randomly meet together, there's a good probability that they either know one another (one degree of separation), or have a common acquaintance (two degrees of separation) or that they each know someone else who has a common acquaintance (three degrees of separation) etc. Well, I of course signed into LinkedIn to see if Her Majesty was already connected to me – however, she does not even have a LinkedIn page, so I only increased my degrees of frustration!

But then came another "Aha moment", the creative solution – I decided I would write directly to the Queen and make mention of the people I knew who *did* have connections to her in an effort to make a direct connection for myself. Perhaps you are rolling your eyes right now – I mean, how many people must write to the Queen every day? Why would my letter stand a chance of standing out from the rest? Good – you are getting the hang of asking questions!

I asked myself the same questions. The approach I took was to make use of the research I had done on the Queen to create a more compelling letter.

What actually went into the letter will be disclosed in the chapter *Attitude – Be Thorough*. On reflection, I suppose I could have been even more daring, more creative with what I put in – but I was also certain that my package would be inspected multiple times by the Royal Mail, by Buckingham Palace Security, and by the Queen's staff so I did not want to go overboard – attract attention, yes, but the right attention, not a visit from Scotland Yard!

I was encouraged to learn that my creative efforts were not in vain – I received a personal response directly from the Queen's "Woman of the Bedchamber" (what a loaded title – this is a senior member of the Royal Household who regularly attends to the Queen), aka Baroness Susan Hussey of North Bradley, aka Lady-in-Waiting Hussey, aka Lady Susan Hussey, aka godmother of Prince William, Duke of Cambridge ("Woman of the Bedchamber"). More on her response later.

Chapter 5

ATTITUDE – BE PERSISTENT

In Need Of A Makeover

Being curious and creative are real building blocks for reaching better observations but to make these blocks into something bigger, you need to throw in some unglamorous cement. In terms of asking good questions, the mortar that binds is the attitude of persistence. Without persistence, all the curiosity and creativity can fall apart and amount to very little as your questions return to you without good answers or without any answers at all.

Persistence does suffer though from an image problem. You just have to visualize news reporters who come off as intrusive, aggressive, and just plain rude as they thrust a microphone into someone's face while barking out rapid fire questions relentlessly until they can provoke a juicy sound bite for the six o'clock news. Not a pretty picture but that kind of tenacity and "do whatever it takes" mindset is a critical factor in observation. If you thought the reporter picture was a bit hard to take, consider some other metaphors used to describe those who do not take "no" for an answer and you gain a fuller idea of persistence:

- "Pit bull": a person who "bites down" on some issue and will not let go.

- "Hound": like a pit bull (especially used as a verb, as in "my boss is hounding me to get the report finished").

- "Stalker": a person who relentlessly pursues a subject.

- "Paparazzi": like a stalker but with a camera.

- "Shadow": like a stalker, used often in sports (from football, the cornerback was all over the wide receiver, shadowing him all the way to the locker room!).

- "Nag": a person who keeps on and on until something gets done.

No Pain, No Gain

So the persistent person may not win any popularity contests, but it's usually the persistent one who is rewarded with results.

Continuing with the whole reporter analogy for one more example, let's look at one of the most persistent, no-nonsense TV interviewers, Mike Wallace, who for decades was a high profile correspondent for the CBS news program, *60 Minutes*. According to CBS:

"Wallace's no-holds-barred interviewing technique and enterprising reportage are well known, and his numerous and timely interviews read like a who's who of newsmakers: George H.W. Bush, Ronald and Nancy Reagan, Richard Nixon, John F. Kennedy, Deng Xiaoping, the Ayatollah Khomeini, Menachem Begin, Anwar el-

Sadat, Yasir Arafat, the Shah of Iran, King Hussein, Hafez Assad, Muammar Qaddafi, Itzhak Perlman, Leonard Bernstein, and Johnny Carson among many others" ("60 Minutes").

Trying to engage with sharp tongued politicians and glib talking entertainers requires skill - and lots of perseverance. During an interview with the famous American playwright, Arthur Miller (author of "Death of a Salesman") Mr. Wallace once asked Mr. Miller to reflect on his long career:

[Mr. Wallace] "You ever think about an epitaph?"

[Mr. Miller, dismissively] "Epitaph? Never gave it a moment's thought."

Now at this point what question or comment would you make? Mr. Miller's curt response would typically shut down further inquiry along that line, but the persistent Mr. Wallace did not retreat, and instead pressed on the attack, replying without blinking:

[Mr. Wallace] "[well then] give it a moment" (Wallace and Gates 262).

I gained an insight on persistence through an over-simplifed comparison of marketing and sales. A curious or creative person could create a stunning media campaign with all the bells and whistles to "wow" a prospect (that's marketing). A persistent person will stick with the prospect, asking questions to surface needs, pain points, objections, and price expectations until the prospect is ready to make the purchase (that's sales). Clearly you need both halves. I often remark that marketing "creates demand" and sales "fulfills demand". The same goes for observation: Curiosity and creativity create an opening through unique and probing questions and persistence drives all of this until there is fulfilment through a satisfactory answer.

Walk The Line

There is, though, a boundary between persistence and poor taste, between persisting and being obnoxious, between sticking with it and being told where to stick it. Some of the answers to this balancing act have been mentioned already or will come in the following chapters, for example:

- *Attitude: Be Creative* – If you persistently ask the same question the same way over and over again, your audience will become desensitized to your query, so you may need to rephrase or come at your question from a completely different angle.

  I was once stuck overnight in an airport in Manaus, Brazil. One very frustrated passenger kept badgering the gate attendant (who was a Portuguese speaker – this was Brazil after all) with the same question in very loud English "When will the plane arrive?" This passenger should have observed the language barrier and the scarcity of accurate information and rephrased the question to ask something like "Que podemos pedir para mais informações" (translation: "Who can we ask for more information?").

- *Preparation: Do Your Homework* – If you are not prepared for a particular situation, you may be pushing hard for a response that cannot come because you lack some critical knowledge. I remember way back (I mean way back) in high school I was working on a math problem. This will sound very geeky, but I was trying to trisect an angle with only a ruler and compass. In earthly language, this means trying to divide an angle, like a sixty degree angle into three exactly equal parts of twenty degrees each, using only those two tools found in every student's geometry set.

I figured this should be possible, especially since students are always (or used to always be) taught to bisect (divide in two equal parts) an angle using these same tools. My math teacher even dangled a carrot, saying I would earn a PhD if I could solve this problem – heady stuff for a teenager. So I went at it for days (and nights), asking myself over and over, "How can this be solved?" I had no lack of persistence, but I hadn't done my homework. It is mathematically impossible to solve the trisection problem. In this case persistence did not pay off.

- *Preparation: Choose the Right Person* - If you are asking the *wrong* person a question, ratcheting up your intensity in the name of persistence will get you nowhere in a hurry. For example, if you are a salesperson, you can dutifully ask a purchasing agent "When will my sale close?" until you are blue in the face, but you really should be asking the end user with the budget that question. Optimism sometimes overtakes salespeople who report that a deal is going to close - that it is just "stuck in purchasing".

Keep Your Eye On The Prize

But once you understand that being persistent is neither a license for being a pest nor a substitute for all the other principles in this book, you can harness persistence and see amazing results. I remember the first big sale I ever closed. I was working in a software startup as a product developer (that's a fancy insider name for a programmer), surrounded by very smart technologists. There was only one problem – no one was spending time selling the products we developed. Unexpectedly, I was tapped to give sales a try.

Instinctively, I began asking myself some *questions* like "What city should I consider first?" and "What industry should I target?"

The answer came to me – I should go after New York City and call on banks. Over the years this has become my default starting point whenever selling a new product. It's not so much the hype around New York as it is the cold hard fact that it is one of, if not the best sales territories in the world, so you seldom go wrong by starting there.

I did some research and decided I'd call Chase Manhattan Bank (now JPMorgan Chase & Co.). But whom did I know there? No one. So I called the bank's general phone number and spoke to an operator. Thus began a long lesson in persistence as I went from person to person (or voice mail to voice mail), day after day, navigating through various departments. I never became discouraged as I looked at this as a chess game – my job was to ask the right questions to reach the right person and whomever was on the other side of the phone had the job of trying to block me (or so I felt).

Somehow by asking questions I finally got to a VP in Global Bank (the investment bank). He happened to have an ongoing project that needed the software that I was trying to sell, so he connected me with his technical team who trialed the product and found it just might do what they needed it to do. Relief!

Several months had passed since my first call with the general operator and it was time to close the sale. A short plane ride to LaGuardia and a very bumpy taxi ride into midtown Manhattan ushered me into the bank's offices on Park Ave., just a few blocks south of the iconic Waldorf Astoria Hotel and Central Park.

For the first time I finally met the VP who sponsored the initial trial. Despite my lack of experience the meeting went well but when I asked him for a purchase order he told me he had no budget for our software. The world stopped revolving while I took this in. Being new to sales I did not quite know how to respond so I did not. I was numb but I thanked him for the meeting and dejectedly turned around with my colleague to leave. I remember taking about four or five steps when persistence kicked in and instinctively I wheeled around and called out to him as he was walking away "What if I let you use the software for free?"

Now if you are a sales professional you are probably shaking your head. I did not know if the VP was negotiating or playing "chicken", but I clearly blinked first. But after all those months of hard work, persistence would not allow me to give up. Thankfully, the VP agreed on the spot to continue to use the software on those no-cost terms.

A few more months passed and this whole new sales thing started to look pretty bleak. There were no sales despite a lot of effort in cold calling. Senior management was asking me some pretty tough questions when suddenly the fax machine started clacking. Right then and there, in the middle of this status meeting, came a purchase order from Chase Manhattan Bank for over a quarter of a million dollars. We were all stunned. Then relieved. Then overjoyed. Thus began my unintended career in sales. I believe that first sale was due to persistence (certainly it wasn't from experience) – from sticking with the bank's telephone operator and clawing all the way up.

Stubborn To The End

What makes a person persistent? I do not have a sure-fire formula but from my observation of people, stubbornness is necessarily part of the equation. This trait is usually seen as negative – stubborn people can dig in their heels and frustrate others through an unwillingness to budge or yield. Yet every weakness can be a strength and every strength can be a weakness.

To me, which side of the ledger stubbornness falls on comes down to the position being held. If someone is stubborn in the face of information that flatly proves the position wrong, then stubbornness is a weakness. However, if the position is well supported by factual information, or if the refuting of the position is itself unsupported, then stubbornness can be a strength.

In the 2008 film *Flash of Genius*, Greg Kinnear portrays engineer Robert Kearns, a real-life entrepreneur who invented the variable speed car windshield wiper. In this true story, Mr. Kearns' invention is manufactured in Ford and Chrysler vehicles without his permission, so the movie recounts the multi-year patent infringement lawsuit that Mr. Kearns launched. In the process, the inventor estranged himself from his wife and children but in the end his persistence pays off morally and financially as he wins his lawsuit. Mr. Kearns' stubbornness was based on a position of truth, hence, while the lengths he went to were arguably too extreme, he epitomized the good that persistence can bring.

Persistence and the Queen

In the previous chapter I hinted that I had received a personal response back from the Queen's "Woman of the Bedchamber" (do not even ask, just go back one chapter for a refresher of who stands behind this intriguing title).

Well if the quest for Her Majesty was simply to collect memorabilia from Buckingham Palace I was off to a good start. However, to get closer to the Queen would demand a lot of persistence. Not unlike my experience with Chase Manhattan Bank, I found myself navigating through an organization chart, but this time a world-wide one with lots of government red tape.

First I went to the source and called Buckingham Palace – their general operator phone number is listed online. I had done some prior research (more in the chapter *Preparation: Do Your Homework*) and so asked to be put through to the Palace Information Office. The operator asked about the nature of my enquiry – I at first stumbled (something about that proper British accent and the realization that I was actually speaking to someone in the Palace unglued me) and so I squeaked out a meek question "I am sending Her Majesty a book and would like to know if I could confirm the mailing address."

Well, at least I did not ask about the weather. But after the operator politely recited the London mailing address the call was over. But due to persistence my quest was just gathering momentum. Next I figured I should also call up the Governor General of Canada – after all, he is the Queen's official representative in Canada (where I live). In case you did not learn this in history class, Canada is a constitutional monarchy wherein Queen Elizabeth II is Canada's official Head of State. In practice, we govern our own affairs but legally, legislation that is passed by our Parliament requires royal assent by the Queen through her representative, the Governor General.

That concludes our mini-history lesson. Again the Internet furnished the general phone number for the Governor General at his residence at Rideau Hall in Ottawa, Canada's capital, so I was on the phone again. This time I chose to ask about the Queen's next visit to Canada – I had been too late for the 2010 visit so I was hoping she was due for another visit soon. You see, if your aim is to meet the Queen, when better than during a visit to your own country – saves me the airfare and travel expenses! The operator referred me over to the Department of Canadian Heritage, a federal government agency responsible for the preservation and advancement of all things Canadian, including royal visits.

Did I mention earlier that stubbornness is part of persistence? When I called up Canadian Heritage, I was sent back to the Governor General's office for matters related to the Queen. At least I did learn in this little back-and-forth shuffle that while I missed the 2010 visit to Canada, the year 2012 marks the Diamond Jubilee of Her Majesty – her sixtieth anniversary as Queen of Canada. That little fact stoked my creativity, curiosity, persistence – you name it – I became more determined to try to find a way to meet the Queen in that auspicious year.

Chapter 6

ATTITUDE – BE THOROUGH

Details, Details

In his autobiography *Larry King, My Remarkable Journey*, Mr. King recounts his love of baseball. He was a die-hard Brooklyn Dodgers fan (the Dodgers moved to Los Angeles in 1958) who would line up to be among the first into the ballpark to watch the Dodgers take batting practice before a game (41-46).

Mr. King in part attributed his unique and successful interviewing style to being thorough: "I learned to pay *attention to details* [italics added] through baseball" (44). He was such a rabid fan that he memorized statistics about the players and the team: "Statistics was something else baseball gave me that would help later on when I was a broadcaster ... Where I grew up, statistics were ammunition" (53).

As we learned with persistence in the last chapter, as you work on developing your question-asking skills, you will find that some of the foundational attitudes behind better observation are simply good old fashioned character traits - like being thorough. Our parents and our teachers have tried to drum these values into us from childhood, using sports and homework as object lessons. Mr. King learned life-long lessons through baseball. For others it could just have easily been from washing the dishes after dinner.

You see, you might still feel tentative about being able to develop creative ability (though I did suggest ways that you can improve in this area) but you should have no such qualms about learning to be persistent or thorough – these are gritty traits that are entirely up to you to exhibit, and you can and must possess these to be successful in any pursuit.

Check Your Work

Here's a case in point. Being a math geek (Full disclosure: before working in the software business I was briefly a college math lecturer, and before that, a math major), I know that those who struggle with math often complain that subjects like algebra have no earthly value. I disagree by the way (just deciding whether a "buy one get the second item at half price" sale on shoes is a good deal or not requires algebra). Think about the number one rule of math you were taught in primary school – "always check your work". This is why you are always supposed to show your "rough work" on a math test – you can double check how you arrived at your answer.

If you learned to check your work doing algebra, then you would have learned to apply that same principle when filling out application forms for a student loan, paying income taxes, buying a car, or even picking a spouse.

Maybe the math analogy isn't working for you because, well, you just hate math. Let's take an example from police investigation, Hollywood style. From the popular TV series, *CSI: Crime Scene*

Attitude – Be Thorough 65

Investigation, the Las Vegas-based investigators are portrayed as masters of being thorough – no details, however minute, seem to escape them.

In Episode Ten, "Sex, Lies, and Larvae", from Season One, lead forensic scientist Dr. Gil Grissom (played by William Petersen) examines a body covered with insects ("CSI: Crime Scene Investigation (season 1)").

"In what Grissom calls 'linear regression', the time of death can be determined by the type and age of insects on the body. Examine what insects are present, determine their current life stage, and count backward to when the first eggs were laid, and you'll have the time of death" (Cortez and Wilson 78).

If you do not like math then let me tell you that I do not like bugs – but being detail-oriented and thorough always leads to better observation. And in Hollywood, this always adds up to a nice clean wrap up in a police show.

The Next Witness

I have a few more convincing examples of the value of being thorough – it seems that these also come from a law/crime/law enforcement world – not surprising when you think about it because criminals are often very attuned to observing little details but it's often little details that also lead to their arrest. As mentioned in the opening chapter, we want to learn from the "observation professionals" – interviewers, doctors, lawyers, investigators, interrogators, and yes, even criminals.

In *Cross-Examination – A Practical Handbook*, author George Colman instructs fellow lawyers on the art of digging out facts from unwilling or unwitting people in the courtroom by concentrating on details. Part of the challenge for those who are not sticklers is that minor details seem ... well ... they seem minor!

Mr. Colman teaches lawyers that "Even the unattractive looking ducklings which seem to swim on, or slightly outside, the periphery of what is important, should receive some attention. They may turn into swans" (32).

To prove the point, Mr. Colman cites an example on questioning minor details about a document entered into evidence. He suggests that questions about the watermark, ink, etc. may lead to a document expert determining that the document is not authentic and hence inadmissible evidence.

From real trial proceedings came another example. An employee was suing his employer in a dispute over vacation leave. The employee claimed that the employer had agreed to give him six weeks of vacation once the employee was married. As evidence, the employee produced a letter that was alleged to be evidence of the mutual agreement. The employee testified that the letter had been typed up by his manager's secretary. However, upon cross-examination, the lawyer for the defendant (the employer) was able to show by examining the margin inset that the manager's secretary always used a 1.25" margin whereas the letter presented as evidence had a 1.5" margin. Such minute detail caused the case of the plaintiff (the employee) to unravel (32-36).

Get Some Exercise

Take a look around you right now. Maybe you are sitting in a coffee shop – take in the details, count the number of muffins in the display case by the cash register, close your eyes and take in the aroma – my children always know if I've been in a Starbucks or a Tim Hortons because that coffee shop smell clings to your clothes.

A simple way to become more thorough is to force yourself to look at *attributes* (more on this in the chapter *Jump Start With Attributes*). Basically, everything has a set of defining attributes or identifiers. Remember the start of this book? I'm a stair-counter. Every time I'm on a stairwell I just count the steps. A bit compulsive perhaps, but the most obvious attribute of a stairwell is how many steps it has.

Try this little exercise. Below are some objects – you list the basic attributes or identifiers – the details that would allow you to remember something useful about the objects:

TABLE 6-1 Listing Attributes (Exercise)

Object	Attributes
Cake in a bakery	
Car on the street	
Bank Branch	

Here's what I came up with:

TABLE 6-2 Listing Attributes (Solution)

Object	Attributes
Cake in a bakery	Flavour (e.g. chocolate, carrot) Shape (e.g. round, rectangular) Colour Icing (did it have any) Occasion (birthday, anniversary, etc.) Price
Car on the street	Make (e.g. Ford, Hyundai, BMW) Model (e.g. Focus, Tucson, X5) Colour Style (e.g. sedan, SUV, van) Doors (e.g. 3, 4, hatchback) Glass (e.g. tinted)
Bank Branch	Affiliation (e.g. TD, HSBC, Citibank) Tellers (e.g. how many) Location ATMs (e.g. how many) Chairs in reception area (e.g. what colour) Hours of operation

When we look at the chapter *Jump Start With Attributes*, we'll see that there may not be a right or wrong answer – each person will think of different defining identifiers for any given object or situation. The key is simply to start to think about attributes – this will train your mind to become more detailed.

What's Left

Come to think of it, what attributes come to mind when you think of left-brained people (the kind of people who are always thinking about attributes in the first place!)?

According to that Left Brain-Right Brain survey we did earlier, the labels tend to be ("Right Brain vs. Left Brain Creativity Test"):

TABLE 6-3 Left Brain vs. Right Brain Attributes

Left Brain	Right Brain
Linear	Holistic
Sequential	Random
Symbolic	Concrete
Logical	Intuitive
Verbal	Nonverbal
Reality-based	Fantasy-oriented

I, being of the Left Brain persuasion, would like to propose a simpler set of attributes – namely the labels I hear most often pinned to us "lefties" – these would be:

- detail-oriented

- process-oriented

My intention isn't to try to re-wire your brain in case you tend to be right-brained. Moreover, I am hardly trying to extol the virtues of being left-brained. Many a time I've been told in no uncertain terms what a liability it is to be so "anal" in details and processes! Nonetheless, in the area of improving observations and question-asking ability by being more *thorough*, I would dare say that left-brained people have a slight advantage by predisposition.

Well, now that all those disclaimers are out, it is possible for *everyone* to get better at observing details - training yourself to think about attributes as we started to do above is a good first step. Learning to think about processes is a bit like playing chess. The legendary chess masters think many moves ahead, working out combinations in their brain like a computer. Specific to our purpose of becoming better at observing, the best way to start to think in processes is to decide on the objective of the questions you are asking or planning to ask, and then trying to work out a short sequence of specific questions to get you to that objective (much like plotting your sequence of moves in a chess match to capture your opponent's king). Later in this book is a chapter devoted to this topic, *Preparation – Have A Specific Objective*.

Scams Are Well Planned

Earlier in this book I had referred to Frank Abagnale, who was a daring and cunning "con man". Among his many "cons", Mr. Abagnale had posed as a Pan Am (airline) pilot, a pediatrician, a Harvard lawyer, and a college professor, bilking people and companies for over USD$2.5 million dollars (this was back in the 1960s).

Mr. Abagnale worked his first scam posing as a pilot by calling Pan Am's purchasing department claiming that his pilot's uniform had been stolen. The purchasing department naively directed him to the airline's uniform supplier without further questioning (talk about poor observation) and so Mr. Abagnale took possession of a Pan Am pilot's uniform (*Catch Me If You Can* 39). Next, Mr. Abagnale misled an ID card printing company, passing himself off as an employee of a fictitious airline searching for a new printing supplier for its ID cards. The printer fell for the ruse and made up some sample airline pilot ID cards for Mr. Abagnale to examine for quality. He pocketed the ID cards, then took decals from Pan Am model airplane kits to make authentic looking Pan Am ID cards.

Armed with his new uniform and ID, he subsequently went on many free flights on different carriers since airlines offered courtesy seats to pilots regardless of which airline employed them. On one occasion Mr. Abagnale was invited into the cockpit of an airborne plane and offered the controls!

But Mr. Abagnale was not just looking for free flights – he wanted free money. He later became a cheque swindler, writing and cashing bad cheques and amassing a fortune. Mr. Abagnale cites the reasons for his success as a check fraudster: "Observation is a skill that can be developed, but I was born blessed with the ability to pick up on details and items the average man overlooks" (*Catch Me If You Can* 146).

So be warned. Criminals can be very skilled at observing, and they choose unwitting victims who do not possess these skills. Fraud-based crime is rampant. A vivid example of the criminal use of observation skills is found in how Mr. Abagnale perpetrated cheque scams. He noticed in the late 1960s, that bank deposit slips could be filled out without specifying the actual bank account number - name and address were all the bank required (in case you do not know what a "bank deposit slip" is, bank customers used to have to fill out a paper form to make a deposit, indicating the amount of each cheque, or the denomination of each bill being deposited in the case of cash).

Mr. Abagnale stayed in a particular bank for hours observing whether most customers filled out the account number box - few did - so he took a stack of blank deposit slips to his apartment and used press-on numbers (that's self-adhesive labels) to put his own bank account number on the slips. The next day he returned to the bank and placed these modified slips on the counters. Four days later he had over

USD$42,000 in his bank account as victims unwittingly deposited money into his account (*Catch Me If You Can* 146).

There were other "cons" masterminded by Mr. Abagnale, but eventually the FBI caught up with him and he was convicted and imprisoned. Upon his release, he became an anti-fraud adviser with clients from banks and other sectors who relied on his keen observation to expose potential weaknesses that criminals could exploit.

In fact, one of the tips that Mr. Abagnale now shares on his website (www.abagnale.com) is the following: apparently banks number cheques sequentially, so the higher the cheque number, the more likely the cheque belongs to a legitimate person (look at your own cheques – every time you run out of cheques and order more from your bank, you'll probably see that the new cheque numbers pick up where the last one left off). "Con men" will open new bank accounts and order cheques to pass fraudulently (however, since the accounts are new, the cheque numbers will be low). Mr. Abagnale advises that if you receive cheques with low cheque numbers, request additional identification to ensure the authenticity of the cheque (*The Art of the Steal* 33).

Details, details. Are you convinced now? Being thorough is an important attitude that you can develop and leverage in becoming better at observation.

Being Thorough And The Queen

I had promised in the chapter, *Attitude – Be Creative*, that I would let you know what I put in the letter I sent to the Queen to try to somehow arrange to meet with her directly against overwhelming odds. You'll find all the raw research material in the chapter *Preparation – Know Your Audience*. The complete text of the letter is at the close of this chapter.

Knowing that I wouldn't have too many opportunities to make a credible approach (as the saying goes, "you only get one chance to make a first impression") I had to be thorough in this letter, touching on pertinent details and anticipating the steps in the process that might lead to a meeting with the Queen.

Having read a number of books on the Queen and on the Royal Family it was obvious that one detail to dote on is horses - they are a big part of Her Majesty's life. The Queen has her own race horses, she has always aspired to win the English Derby, many horse racing events are named after her (like the "Queen's Plate" in Canada), her only daughter, Princess Anne, is an accomplished equestrian who competed in the 1976 Olympics (the only royal Olympic athlete to date), and for the 2012 Diamond Jubilee, five hundred horses are being assembled as part of a special equestrian show at Windsor Castle. Yes, you'd have to be pretty un-observant to miss this big equine detail.

So the first detail to attend to in my letter had to be the paper it would be written on. I started by creating my own custom stationery – I picked a heavy paper (blue for royalty of course) and then created a specific watermark using an image of an English Derby horse race.

The content of the letter made reference to the friends and relatives that connected me to the Queen (however far removed) in an attempt to create some common bond (the "LinkedIn" idea).

Since I knew she had staff to read her letters and to decide which ones would be forwarded to the Queen, and what response each letter deserved, I had to think about *process* – my letter had to stand out from the thousands of others she would receive so that each Palace staffer who had to review my letter and decide whether to pass it on would actually do so.

To try to improve my odds of receiving a response, I had found out what books she prefers to read in her scant spare time. In general she is not an avid reader but she likes to read Dick Francis novels. Not surprisingly, Dick Francis was an accomplished jockey himself, having ridden for none other than the Queen Mother (i.e. the mother of Queen Elizabeth II) before he retired and became a prolific fiction writer. And the theme of all his mystery books? With titles like *Dead Heat*, *High Stakes*, *Even Money* and *Longshot*, I think you can guess what the common theme is in every book he wrote. So I purchased a brand new hardcover copy of the latest Dick Francis book and sent it along with the letter.

Thinking further through the process I decided I needed to make impressions for her staffers even with the package wrapping. I inserted the letter into a matching blue envelope, and wrapped the book in tartan tissue paper (more royal decor – I had considered buying some extra special tissue paper that had a corgis theme – that's the Queen's favourite dog – but the bill for the book and the postage was already climbing too quickly for a poor writer's budget). I did not use any tape on the tissue paper because, thinking through the process, I knew that multiple people would inspect the package, so tape would end up tearing the tissue paper and leaving a mess – not the right impression.

And just to prove how obsessed I can be with details and process, I inserted a second copy of the letter in the back of the book jacket in case the letter became separated from the book because of all the handling and inspection that would happen.

Even with all that thorough preparation, I knew the likelihood of success was almost zero. Nonetheless, I wanted to be sure that if I failed, it would not be for lack of thorough preparation.

FIGURE 6-1 The Author's Letter To HRH Queen Elizabeth II

May 9, 2011

Her Majesty The Queen
Buckingham Palace
London SW1A 1AA

Your Majesty,

I am writing a book to help children and adults recover the lost art of asking good questions. I volunteer every weekend to work with school-aged children at my local church and throughout my years of teaching, I have found that people young and old have become very unobservant – hence I feel I have a duty to try to equip people to ask good questions, to instil both curiosity and the joy of discovery once more. It is not an easy task.

With the recent royal wedding, I have been trying to practise what I preach by asking friends and family some simple questions about the monarchy. I have been quite stunned to discover how many in my circle have met with Your Majesty's family, for example:

- My niece had the honour of presenting flowers to your Majesty on your most recent visit to Toronto (I have enclosed a photo).
- A dear retired friend had the pleasure of attending one of your garden parties as a foreign student in London in the 1950s – she never had the opportunity to thank you for the kindness.
- This same friend had served as a nurse in London and once was on hand when HRH King George VI was being attended to at the Brompton Hospital.
- Another acquaintance had attended Lakefield College School here in Canada, graduating in the same class as HRH Prince Andrew, The Duke of York.

For someone of Chinese ancestry living his entire life in Canada and having never visited England, I found these connections to be quite special indeed!

In part due to these unexpected connections, you have inspired me to press on with my book. I would be so honoured if Your Majesty would permit me to personally present you with a copy of my book. I dare not presume a private audience, but would humbly ask if I with my wife could bring the book to one of your upcoming Garden Parties?

I have also come to learn that you are a Dick Francis reader, as am I. Should my own book not be completed in time to present, I have enclosed Mr. Francis' latest book as a more than capable placeholder!

Most sincerely,

Albert Lee

Chapter 7

ATTITUDE – BE SKEPTICAL

Cyber Crime

Finally, we come to the last chapter on the attitudes that we need to make better observations and to ask better questions. Think back to your childhood - you may remember being exhorted to "get rid of that negative attitude". Maybe you hated practising piano, or doing homework, or ... you fill in the rest.

But in the case of learning to ask good questions, some negative attitudes can in fact be helpful, even indispensable. Specifically, being skeptical is a key ingredient to asking good questions. In the previous chapter we had already encountered the advice of an expert cross examiner who overturned evidence by paying attention to a document margin inset. Underneath all that thorough sifting was the lawyer's skepticism that the plaintiff was speaking truthfully. That skepticism allowed the lawyer to prepare his cross-examination questions.

In *The Art of the Steal*, by Mr. Abagnale, the former cheque scammer with the Pan Am pilot's uniform warned that the US Federal Trade

Commission (FTC) once discovered that ten percent of donations went to *bogus* charities – that could mean that one of your last ten charitable gifts ended up enriching some crook. This prompted the reformed Mr. Abagnale to advise that "When in doubt, [before donating] always ask for written information about the charity" (*The Art Of The Steal* 115).

There are many legitimate non-profit organizations advocating for very needy causes so I urge you to continue to donate, but do so with some skepticism to confirm the organization's legitimacy. Ask some *questions*. Not long ago a young woman was charged for posing online as a cancer patient. She fooled many unsuspecting donors, including one who apparently funded a "last wish" trip to Disneyland for the fraudster. The ensuing outrage included death threats which prompted court officials to whisk this woman out the back door of the court house (Clairmont).

The Art of the Steal offers us more warnings. One fraud crime begins with a phone offer of low-cost merchandise (e.g. a "free" TV for the price of shipping) in exchange for your credit card number to pay for the shipping. There is no TV on its way to you - this ruse is intended to wrest away your credit card details so someone else can buy TVs on your account (114).

A number of my friends recently gave out their email passwords in response to an Internet scam whereby messages appeared to come from trusted individuals who invited recipients to view a photo sharing website. There are lots of legitimate such sites but be suspicious of those that ask you for your email password. Why do people fall for these schemes? We need a healthy dose of skepticism.

Part of the challenge of taming fraud is that victims do not always share what was learned. Duped individuals feel foolish. Corporations have an image to uphold. It's no longer amateurish online scams about some distressed overseas company requiring your banking information to safeguard a fortune in exchange for a non-existent reward.

Organized crime perpetrates well-constructed, well-executed cyber-crimes.

If you do not protect yourself online you need to start. According to SplashData, a password security software provider, the top twenty-five worst passwords of 2011 are:
- password
- 123456
- 12345678
- qwerty
- abc123
- monkey
- 1234567
- letmein
- trustno1
- dragon
- baseball
- 111111
- iloveyou
- master
- sunshine
- ashley
- bailey
- passw0rd
- shadow
- 123123
- 654321
- superman
- qazwsx
- michael
- football

According to SplashData's website, this "list was compiled from files containing millions of stolen passwords posted online by hackers" ("SplashID Password Manager for Mobile Devices, Mac OS & Windows"). If you are using any of these passwords you need to change them fast. Remember, criminals are usually better at observation than everyone else.

Everything Old Is New Again

Before you start categorizing these frauds as new inventions aimed only at the technologically challenged, consider the following example from the Great Depression era of the 1930s from *Annals of Gullibility – Why We Get Duped and How to Avoid It,* by Stephen Greenspan. The author describes a crime perpetrated by a former farm boy, Oscar Hartzell, who claimed that Sir Francis Drake, the famous English sea explorer in the age of Queen Elizabeth I (not the Queen I am trying to meet), had amassed a fortune as a pirate which was left to an heir, Colonel Drexel Drake.

This Colonel allegedly fell in love with Mr. Hartzell's supposed niece and willingly signed over his very sizeable inheritance to Mr. Hartzell. But alas, Mr. Hartzell needed investors so that he would have the funds required to settle the inheritance in court, whereupon he would naturally provide a healthy return on investment. To make the "con" sound more authentic, Mr. Hartzell claimed that Sir Francis Drake's will was being validated by a "Lord and King's Commission" – who could argue with that (130-133)!

Apparently, most of the investors who hailed from the Midwestern US did not argue. They bought into the scam in part due to their own bias against investing in stocks as an investment vehicle. Mr. Hartzell was able to exploit this bias, which was rooted in the Midwesterners' mistrust of the north-eastern US powers that controlled the stock markets (and I'm sure also on their minds was the fact that the stock market had crashed only a few years earlier in 1929).

Did we not already learn earlier from Mr. Abagnale that criminals are experts in observation whereas victims are not? Mr. Hartzell had swindled his victims so effectively that even when he was deported and eventually put on trial, his Midwestern investors stuck by him, raising money for his defence, and insisting that the trial itself was all staged as part of the US government's cover up of their difficulties in dealing with such a huge financial transaction!

Fight Back

This incredible gullibility could have been averted if some skepticism caused questions to be asked and due diligence to be done. Basic questions like the following should have come out:

- What proof do you have that Colonel Drake really existed?

- What evidence is there that the "Lord and King's Commission" existed (there is no evidence - the "Commission" was made up)?

- Where is the proof that Sir Francis Drake's will was contested (it wasn't)?

- Since Sir Francis Drake had died so long ago, is his will still contestable (England had a twelve year statute of limitations)?

From Bad To Worse

Now at this point you might have the idea that you shouldn't trust anybody. But skepticism is differentiated from cynicism. That's why it's called "healthy skepticism" – it isn't a bad thing that you should reserve judgment on whether some fact or scheme or offer is legitimate. It is prudent to demand some credible and defensible answers by asking some basic probing questions to authenticate claims. To always dismiss every claim outright is not healthy skepticism, it has devolved into unhealthy cynicism.

As an entrepreneur, I always have new business ideas – most of them would probably never fly but being ever the optimist, I suspect some of the ideas are viable. But what I've learned is that the very first question an entrepreneur should ask himself is: "If I have this great idea, then who else already has this idea?" This is an example of healthy self-doubt that leads to proper due diligence - a quick search for what intellectual property lawyers call "prior art", pre-existing evidence like patent applications or published white papers.

Just reflect on some of the major technical advancements in history – the radio, the telephone, the airplane ... you immediately think of Guglielmo Marconi, Alexander Graham Bell, and Wilbur and Orville Wright as the inventors. But did you know that you should also think of Nicola Tesla ("Invention of Radio"), Elisha Gray ("Elisha Gray and Alexander Bell telephone controversy"), and Glenn Curtiss ("Glenn Curtiss")? They were also working on the same inventions at the same time. To convince yourself that you have a *unique* idea is usually wishful, overly optimistic thinking. And as I said, the opposite end of the spectrum – to immediately dismiss the idea since someone else must already have thought of it is overly pessimistic thinking that kills innovation. Entrepreneurs have to live in the middle.

Fight Back, Round Two

You can also arm yourself because it *is possible* to fight back against scammers by asking the right questions. Mr. Abagnale recounts the story of a "con man", posing as the heir to Sir Thomas Lipton's estate, approaching researchers with the offer to give large USD$200 MM research grants in exchange for USD$350K to be held in escrow. "Some of those contacted were resourceful enough to call Unilever [the owner of Lipton Tea] to validate the offer (which was fabricated, and hence they spared themselves from becoming victims)" (*The Art of the Steal* 120).

Attitude – Be Skeptical   83

The CBC (Canadian Broadcasting Corp. – Canada's public broadcaster) aired a TV segment, *Won't Be Fooled Again*, devoted to exposing fraud crimes. Specific to those incessant yet seemingly laughable Nigerian money transfer frauds that people still fall for, here are some questions that the CBC suggested as a first line of defence ("Q & A with Nigerian Scam Con"):

- "First of all, why would anybody want to transfer millions of dollars to you? I mean who are you?"

- "Secondly why can't things go through your bank, why can't your banker get involved, why can't your lawyer get involved right?"

- "The number one thing that's just coming back to me, the number one thing is why can't I meet you — the person should insist on meeting the individual that they're dealing with. Any scammer out there that's worth his salt will not be interested in meeting anyone because there's identification, the police could be following, you could be videotaped, you could be handcuffed right on the spot, so meeting the client is the number 1 thing that a scammer doesn't want. If you insist on a meeting and the scammer insists on not having a meeting that's an immediate tell tale (sic) sign."

Here are some resources to prepare you to fight back against fraud:

- Mr. Abagnale's book gives a sample quiz to identify your vulnerability to identity theft (*The Art of the Steal* 214).

- The Competition Bureau Canada has an online quiz, *Recognize The Scam*: http://www.competitionbureau.gc.ca/eic/site/cb-bc.nsf/eng/03349.html.

- Industry Canada has a Fraud Quiz: http://www.ic.gc.ca/eic/site/oca-bc.nsf/eng/ca01960.html.

The Reference Check Please

Before we leave this chapter, I wouldn't want you to think that the attitude of skepticism is only directed at flushing out crime. If you've ever been involved in the standard job interview process, you'll know that skepticism is essential when validating some of the glowing credentials that appear on candidate resumes.

Before entering the software world I mentioned I had a brief stint as a college math instructor. During the interview, rather than ask typical questions like: "Can you describe your teaching experience?", the interviewer asked me to describe how I would teach fractions to college students (yes, you heard right – fractions). My interviewer knew how to ask better questions to validate whether my *claims* on knowing how to teach were valid.

In my current role as a business strategy consultant to software companies I am often pulled into the interviewing process, particularly to examine sales candidates. There are a lot of good questions to ask references but there are also a lot of standard, low value questions that merely go through the motions.

To apply what we're learning about healthy skepticism, you have to begin with an assumption: every reference for a job candidate is going to be positive. Have you ever applied for a job and asked someone who dislikes you or undervalues you to be your reference? Not likely. Sometimes candidates go so far as to prime their references with good things to say in a reference check (in case they forgot how great the candidate is).

Against this backdrop, the successful interviewer has to approach reference checks with the right questions to draw out a more candid picture of a candidate from a reference that may be reluctant to co-operate. Who says interviewing cannot be fun!

What follows is a compilation of some fairly standard questions that references are asked along with my own assessment of why the question isn't very effective and a suggestion of a better alternative question. If you remember the earlier chapter, *Attitude: Be Creative*, we looked at identifying the "box" - the constraints - so that we could develop targeted questions that went beyond the box.

In a later chapter, *Technique: Have A Specific Objective*, we will take a similar approach of targeting questions, but for a specific objective. Our approach below is similar to that - we are identifying the underlying objective of each question and applying some skepticism to reformulate the question. The aim is to bypass the usual responses so we can decide if we want to hire the candidate.

TABLE 7-1 Improving Interview Reference Check Questions

Standard Question	Why It's Not Effective	Better Question
Comment on his/her ability to be an individual contributor as well as a member of a team.	Every resume claims that the candidate works well individually and on a team. Given that most people are either introverted (someone who recharges by being alone) or extroverted (someone who recharges by being with others), most would work better in one or the other environment but not both. That doesn't preclude that a candidate can thrive in both environments, but we're looking for where the candidate has an edge, so we need to understand the candidate's "natural habitat".	Is the candidate an introvert or an extrovert?
What are his strengths and weaknesses?	The question seems to be striking a balance and opening the way to "get at the dirt". However, many references extol the strengths and downplay or come up	In what area have you seen the most improvement (this forces the reference to agree that improvement is needed, and hence

Attitude – Be Skeptical   87

Standard Question	Why It's Not Effective	Better Question
	empty on weaknesses – or spin by saying that "his only weakness is that he works too hard instead of delegating" – maybe this is true but it's not very helpful to your cause.	exposes weaknesses)?
Describe his/her relationship with his peers, clients, and direct reports.	This question really is often trying to determine how the candidate deals with conflict.	Describe a situation where he was in conflict with a colleague or a business contact, and how the conflict played out (you cannot assume there was resolution)?
How does he handle pressure?	This question is fine and probably is answered with an anecdote, which is also fine. Perhaps it would be even more telling to push to find the candidate's limit of pressure or comfort zone.	Describe a pressure-packed situation that you observed the candidate in and what you think his comfort zone is.

Standard Question	Why It's Not Effective	Better Question
How does he handle criticism?	You are really trying to find out what criticisms have been levelled already and what the candidate is doing about them and how he took the criticisms.	What things were you working on with the candidate to improve on, how did it go, and how did he handle it when you pointed out the deficiencies?
Is he a good communicator?	Everyone has his own way of communicating (e.g. written, oral, with examples, by pictures etc.). Since communication is a two-way exercise, what you really want to know is what style he uses to ensure compatibility.	What is his communication style?
Has he managed people before?	You want to know how he leads people so ask this outright.	What is his leadership style?
[No standard question here, unfortunately]	I find not many ask questions about how a candidate learns – yet learning style is critical as nothing stays the same and good employees need to be able to acquire new skills and knowledge quickly and effectively.	How does he like to learn (e.g. by reading, watching, doing, through examples etc.)?

Standard Question	Why It's Not Effective	Better Question
Comment on his attitude	This question usually results in a lot of sunny words of little value – the best measure of a good attitude is how a candidate does with tasks he hates to do.	What tasks did the candidate like doing most/least – how did the candidate approach these extremes?
Would you hire him/her again and at what level?	This is the ultimate standard question. The reference always says "yes" otherwise the interviewer raises doubts about the candidate's quality. The standard question is really intended to ask the reference the following "knowing what you now know about the candidate, would you hire him again?"	What did you learn about the candidate over the years that you wished you knew at the beginning when you were interviewing him? [I was told recently by a New York Wall St. reference that this was a good question that made him pause and think]

Skepticism and the Queen

Whenever I told people about my quest to meet the Queen, I got this look of surprise, followed by doubt, followed by the question "How are you going to do that?"

I must admit that I surprised myself too when I decided I would go down this path! My next thought was that only powerful, influential, or accomplished people have any hope of meeting Her Majesty. I hadn't done anything worthy of a knighthood and I'd never even been to the Queen's 'hood (i.e. the UK). There was skepticism creeping in but not anxiety.

I'll tell the fuller story in a later chapter, *Preparation – Know Your Audience*, but from my initial research on the Queen I discovered that she does actually meet with "commoners" every year – and not just meeting people handing her flowers along the roadside when she goes out on a royal tour. Usually every year in June and July the Queen hosts a *Garden Party* – three of these are at Buckingham Palace and the fourth is at Holyroodhouse in Edinburgh, Scotland.

FIGURE 7-1 The Queen's Garden Parties

> **The Queen's Garden Parties**
>
> So what exactly goes on at a Garden Party?
>
> - The 8,000 or so invited guests arrive at the Palace by 3PM ("The Guests").
> - The Queen with Prince Philip, the Duke Of Edinburgh and other Royal Family arrive at 4PM.
> - The British National Anthem is played.
> - The Royal Family meet selected guests in specific lanes in the Garden.
> - There is a 400 foot long (120 m) buffet table at which guests eat half a ton of sandwiches and drink 11,000 cups of tea.
> - The Party concludes at 6PM.
>
> ("What Happens at a Garden Party")
>
> - The Garden Parties were first instituted as afternoon "breakfasts" by Queen Victoria in the 1860s.
> - The annual cost of the Parties is about £600,000 (about USD$940,000).
>
> (Hardman 11)

Well, there, I was all set. The Garden Party. Time to book my flight. Except ... who gets to go and how does one go about getting invited? I learned that there are up to a total of thirty thousand people invited to the annual garden parties, with invitees' names put forward by the UK government, British Armed Forces, charities, and societies ("Garden Parties").

Hmm ... not being in any British military service, charity, or society, I had to dig deeper.

Leveraging the previous chapter about being thorough, I learned from the response to my package to Buckingham Palace (the letter and Dick Francis book) that it is the High Commission of Canada in London, which is responsible for choosing which Canadians would be invited to a Garden Party.

From the High Commission I asked more questions and found out that of the thirty thousand guests invited each year, only about *two hundred* guests are chosen from Canada, where I live. Remember, I'm a math guy, so that's less than 1 percent, about 0.67 percent of the total. Not great odds.

That was a bit sobering – but I did not give up. Part of the reason I had sent the Queen the latest Dick Francis novel was to try to increase my visibility with the royal apparatus to try to influence the selection process. In all my correspondence with the High Commission I always made reference to the letter I received from Lady Hussey for the same reason.

All of these actions stemmed from a healthy skepticism that the High Commission for the second longest reigning British monarch (Queen Victoria is the longest) in history would pick an ordinary person out of the over 34 million Canadians who could apply for consideration. I had to remain skeptical but undeterred.

Chapter 8

PREPARATION – HAVE A SPECIFIC OBJECTIVE

What's Your Point?

Take a deep breath and congratulate yourself – you just finished the five principles from the Attitude segment. Let's remind ourselves of the big picture again:

FIGURE 8-1 The APT Principles

A ATTITUDE	Be Curious Be Creative Be Persistent Be Thorough Be Skeptical
P PREPARATION	Have A Specific Objective Do Your Homework Know Your Audience Choose The Right Person Don't Assume
T TECHNIQUE	Watch Your Language Listen Actively Soften Up Your Audience Ask Short Simple Questions Look for Inconsistencies

Starting with this chapter we now move to the Preparation segment. David Frost, the intrepid interviewer of former president Richard Nixon declared that "The goal of any good interviewer is truth" (139).

Maybe that sounds a bit lofty coming from the media industry whose goal is viewership and advertising revenue, but the point is that there needs to be a point i.e. preparation step number one is all about having a specific objective to your line of questioning so that you streamline and focus your queries to meet whatever that objective is.

Regarding the Nixon interviews, Mr. Frost: had a **specific objective** in his interview questions: "One issue I [Mr. Frost] wanted to work through as a group was what it would take to prove Nixon's guilt

Preparation – Have A Specific Objective   95

[conspiracy to obstruct justice] if this were a criminal conspiracy trial" (100).

Do you ever hear interviews where the interviewer is asking aimless questions that do not draw out any insight? Recently a news show host was talking to a woman who had joined protests in Cairo, Egypt. The previous day the army executed a brutal show of force and was caught on video assaulting a woman protester – she was dragged on the pavement by her clothes until she was half naked, was hit repeatedly with truncheons and then stomped on. With this horrific backdrop the interviewer asked her female guest if that violent incident caused any other women to think twice about protesting. Duh. What do you think? Inane questions like that drive me to distraction.

I know in most of the interviews I've ever participated in on either side of the table that "candid moments" tend to be highly orchestrated, scripted affairs. Marketing and spin are not usually very spontaneous – they're just staged to look that way. The questions are often sent ahead of time (and in some cases the very questions to be asked are specified by the guest to the interviewer) and the responses sound like it too.

Not so with Mike Wallace of *60 Minutes*. Mr. Wallace's style was investigative reporting – he liked to stir things up and throw quotes from other sources at his guest *with the objective* of eliciting a response. You can probably tell from the other Mike Wallace sound bites encountered in earlier chapters, but just in case, here is another example.

Mr. Wallace would often ask questions to try to get inside the brain of his guest, to draw out opinions, and thoughts. In a 1957 interview, Mr. Wallace was interviewing Governor Orval Faubus of Arkansas at a time when the forced integration of black and white students was a divisive issue. To satisfy his objective, Mr. Wallace directly pressed three times for personal reflection from the Governor:

Governor, what is your *opinion* [italics added] of the crowds of white adults who gather outside Central High School each weekday morning? ...

What do you *think* [italics added] of these people ...

Personally [italics added], do you favour Negro and white children sitting together in classrooms? (Wallace 74-75)

Substance Over Style

Now that's not to say that a combative, "in-your-face" style is the only way to flush out candour.

Larry King employs a more "folksy", conversational style, which serves to relax a guest so that Mr. King can then suddenly surprise his counterpart *with the objective* of satisfying the host's curiosity. David Frost used a strategic, directive, cross-examination style with Mr. Nixon *with the objective* of eliciting a confession. Dr. Jerome Groopman has a collegial, encouraging discovery style that he has honed *with the objective* of coaxing out what is really causing his patients concern.

TABLE 8-1 Communication Style and Objectives

Speaker	Style	Objective
Mike Wallace	Combative	Elicit opinion
Larry King	Conversation	Satisfy curiosity
David Frost	Cross-examination	Prove guilt
Dr. Jerome Groopman	Collegial	Discovery

So it's not about your communication style — however you interact with people is fine. It's all about having a specific objective so that your style will have substance.

It's been more than a few chapters since I made my rant so here it is again:

> **Ask the right question, get the right answer.**
> **Ask the wrong question, get the wrong answer.**

And if you have no objective, then how do you know if you are right or wrong? You've probably heard the lament that if you have no goal you will hit it every time. Think of it this way: the word "question" has "quest" as its first syllable. A quest is a hunt, a search that is very directive. So know what you are hunting for from the get-go.

Objective Evidence

Again from my experiences in selling enterprise software, I have witnessed often that those without a specific objective can talk to a prospective customer and wrongly conclude that there is *no* opportunity simply because the seller asked the wrong questions.

Suppose you are selling widgets to Citibank. You head over to their midtown Manhattan office to figure out if they have any potential to be your customer. An IT manager greets you. What question do you ask?

Maybe you start down the line of teasing out some pain points that your marketing person told you that your products address. That's fine. Maybe you ask if they have any money to spend. What? Citibank? Money to spend? You know what I mean, of course they have tons of money — maybe it's your money. But do they have a budget for your widgets? That's a good question too. Me? I like to let the prospect first tell me about the details of their operations.

Most humans like to establish their significance. We like titles. Our resumes are varnished with our achievements (which is why the previous chapter raised the need for healthy skepticism in reviewing reference checks during interviews). Corporate types describe themselves based on how close they are to the CEO in the org chart. So I would do some homework (remember that chapter?) and find some executives in the reporting chain and ask the IT manager if he reports directly into one of those executives. I will write down every word that comes back in the answer because it will tell me all the people I have to meet to close a sale. These org chart details also help me to assess how much influence and authority this manager has.

But that's not my real objective. I want to size up the sales opportunity to know how much effort to put in. Will this be a strategic sale (meaning low revenue but a door opener to more sales), a one-time sale, or an enterprise sale (in the business we call these "all-you-can-eat" deals because the customer pays for a right to deploy as many software licenses as they want up to some ceiling)?

The software I once sold was infrastructure-related (you needed it to run your business, but it was a cost centre item) so I would ask the IT manager how many servers (i.e. high-end physical computers for running critical services – web, data, messaging, and applications) he had to manage. From that simple question I could forecast the total revenue potential (one time and recurring) and how high up the customer chain I would need to go to make a sale. *That* was my objective.

If our sales team told me that the customer wouldn't disclose their server count I would coach them. As I said, people like to assert their significance. If they block your objective, ask the question differently so that you can meet your objective. Simply guess out loud how many servers the IT manager has under his jurisdiction. Better yet, guess on the *low* side. Almost always the manager will correct you because the server count is a point of personal pride. And technical people are numbers and detail-oriented so if you are way off they tend to set you straight.

There is usually a way to get the information you are looking for if you have the objective firmly in mind and you employ some creativity to ask the right question.

Proof Point: Toilet Talk

Allow me to share another experience from the business trenches. When I co-founded a software startup in 2005, we were feeling all the ups and downs of a fledgling technology company. We had closed our first round of venture capital (VC) and we were pushing hard to get out our first software release. If you've never worked for a startup let me warn you that most startups fail (the anecdotal statistic is a 90% failure rate). Even when you manage to attract funding (which after the tech bubble burst in the year 2000 is considerably harder than sketching a business plan on the back of the legendary napkin) you have a high corporate mortality rate.

And when you attract capital, you also attract the scrutiny of investors who now own a good chunk of your business and who sit on your governing board to safeguard their investment. We had a commitment tied to the release of more funding based on closing our first sale. Well, the deadline came and went, and with it came a near death experience for the company and for me as its CEO. The pressure became intense as we had weekly calls with the investor to explain the state of our sales pipeline.

Fortunately, we gained the interest of one of the biggest investment banks on Wall Street (and yes, this bank still exists). We flew senior staff to Manhattan to guide a field trial of our nascent software and progress was steady. The critical juncture came when the bank decided to pay us a visit in Toronto. A Managing Director came up with about five or six other senior team members. They asked to see our office (I think they had their doubts that we even had an office). We met all day in productive meetings. But by about 3PM we were still just talking – there was no deal. We needed a deal.

Just before the meeting was due to end, the Managing Director arose to use the restroom. I looked at his empty chair and then made a split-second decision. I stood up and headed to the restroom too. I had a specific objective, but it was not biological. There was no one else in the restroom but the Managing Director and me. He was literally doing his business so I decided to try to save ours.

I asked him then and there if he would give us a purchase order. I told him how much it would have to be for us to continue supporting the bank's field trial. And as we walked out of the restroom together we had a deal! Unorthodox? Yes. Repeatable? Probably not. But if you have a specific objective you will ask the right questions until you succeed.

Entrapment

Lest you think that I coast from win-to-win, let me assure you that whatever I learned about good observation came as much from failure as success. I remember my very first university job placement interview. Having enrolled in a program that integrated real work experience with academics, every four or so months, all of us "co-op" students had to suit up in business attire (I still rode my bicycle though) and go through interviews with companies that supported the program.

My first such interview was with IBM – still the world's biggest information technology company. In those days as a teenaged freshman, I had not begun to hone the art of asking (or answering) good questions. The interview was progressing really well by my estimates. It began with a review of my high school grades which were top tier. While I was riding that wave the interviewer then lowered the boom. She asked me "Why are your grades in university so much lower than in high school?" I must have stammered out something but I do not remember what I said. The interviewer was prepared and she had an objective. She gave me the interview in the first place so I do not think my lower university performance was a big deterrent – I believe she had an objective to find out what I was made of, how I thought on my feet, to see if the lower grades were an aberration or a trend of things to come.

I never got the chance. I didn't get the job, and ended up working my first work term in a can manufacturing plant. It was still a good experience, but it was no IBM.

Breaking The Fifth

In *Police Interrogation*, author R. Woods shares some tricks of the trade that help police detectives meet their specific objective. Mr. Woods states that "[Interrogation is defined as] the formal and official examination of a person by the use of questioning and persuasion *for the purpose of inducing him to reveal intentionally concealed information* [italics added], usually self-incriminatory in nature" (2).

The following techniques disclosed by Mr. Woods make it clear that they are well matched to an interrogator's objective:

TABLE 8-2 Interrogation Techniques

Interrogation Technique	Explanation
"The 'You Did Nothing Wrong' Approach" (7)	Basically, you try to convince the suspect that you believe they are innocent so that they have no need to worry about giving you all kinds of details about the crime. Once suspects are lulled into a false sense of security, they tend to say too much.
"The 'Speak Now or Regret it Later' Approach" (9)	Assumes the suspect is guilty, so the suspect is better off disclosing the facts now than later. TV police dramas often use this line of dialogue, like "If you co-operate you might get off easier in front of a judge ..."
"Ego Manipulation" (10)	Deflate a suspect's ego by intentionally underestimating the suspect's abilities so they will correct the interrogator and blurt out the facts. For example, an interrogator might tell the suspect that the suspect isn't smart enough to plan a bank robbery and hence must be innocent; surprisingly, the suspect may end up blurting out crime evidence to prove the interrogator wrong. A variation is to inflate a suspect's ego through the use of flattery with the same objective.

Interrogation Technique	Explanation
"Good Cop – Bad Cop" (11)	This one is commonly used in more than just police interrogation. Two interrogators face a suspect; one interrogator advocates for the suspect and the other accuses the suspect. The theory is that the "bad cop" softens up the suspect, and then the suspect opens up to the "good cop".
"Extension" (12)	Basically, the interrogator befriends the suspect, tries to empathize with why the suspect had reason to commit the crime. For example, the interrogator might say "Your neighbour sounds terrible, it sounds like he got what he deserved…" Following this a confession may be forthcoming.

Gordon MacKinnon defines in *Investigative Interviewing* that "[investigative interviewing is] a conversation with a purpose [i.e. a specific objective]. Someone has information – your job, as the interviewer, is to have them give you that information" (11).

One of the most typical investigative questions is: "Do you know why you're here?" (MacKinnon 12). Mr. MacKinnon also lets us in on a secret. The most important question in investigation is simply "What happened?" He claims that "All other investigative questions flow from these two simple words" (MacKinnon 15).

From Cross-Examination – A Practical Handbook, author George Colman reveals that in cross-examination, it is critical to "have a clear objective for the questioning". In other words, "[to] be fully familiar with the issues in the suit ... so that he [the cross examiner] will have a clear appreciation of what he wants or can hope to obtain, from the witnesses" (25).

Mr. Colman goes on to enumerate some key objectives:

- "To demonstrate that a witness has been mistaken on one or more points of evidence, or is biased" (5).

- "To show that material points have been omitted or stressed inadequately" (5).

- "To assist in the administration of justice by revealing the truth to the court" (4).

- "In special cases to show that the witness is a deliberate liar" (6).

The Bible Of Good Questions

Examples of good questions built on clear objectives can be found if you know where to look for them. In the Bible, there are some real incisive questions that can leave you amazed. You may have never read the Bible nor care for it, but so much of our heritage, culture, language, and values come from the Bible, so if for no other reason than historical context, I encourage you to read it.

In one account, the local authorities in Jerusalem are trying to discredit Jesus. They must have excelled in math and logic because they cooked up a real brain teaser. The authorities cornered Jesus and asked him if they should pay taxes to the Romans.

Now if you know your history, in the first century, Jerusalem was part of the Roman Empire. The locals however were not thrilled with the Roman occupation and even less thrilled about paying taxes to the Romans. But Jesus was going around stirring things up by calling people to return to God.

So how would Jesus respond? Don't pay Caesar? That would advocate rebellion against authority – not very godly. Pay Caesar? That would advocate submission to a human ruler who forced his subjects to worship Caesar over God – also not palatable.

Jesus' response? He asked "Whose portrait is this? And whose inscription? [answer: Caesar's] … Give to Caesar what is Caesar's, and to God what is God's" (Mt 22:20-21, New International Version). Wow. He asked an incisive question that exposed the motives of the local authorities who were trying to trip him up with a no-win scenario. That's because Jesus could read the authorities. He had an objective to expose, and his response did just that.

Have A Specific Objective And The Queen

I remember so clearly when I first decided to apply all the APT Principles in this book to reaching someone significant. At first I thought of US President Barack Obama. However, with all due respect to Mr. Obama, I had to factor in that with 2012 being an election year, he might not be in office by the time I made my approach.

Then all of a sudden the idea came to me … I decided I wanted to try to *speak* with the Queen - on the phone no less. Why the Queen? She is arguably the highest profile public figure of our time, and for many decades before that. Moreover many of us had the royal family on the brain because not long ago in April 2011 the world witnessed the wedding of HRH Prince William and Catherine (Kate) Middleton, now the Duchess of Cambridge. And 2012 is the Queen's Diamond Jubilee (sixty years on the throne). Plus I live in Canada, one of the Commonwealth nations for whom HRH Queen Elizabeth II is the Head of State, the Queen of Canada.

So I was settled on finding a way to speak with Her Majesty. Not so easy. As I thought about this more soberly, it dawned on me that trying to speak to her by "cold calling" would be a touch more challenging than cold calling Chase Manhattan Bank. All the privacy laws in corporate America couldn't come close to the fiercely guarded privacy of the royal family.

In an earlier chapter I'd already shared the dead-end I hit attempting to directly connect to the Queen through LinkedIn or Facebook. I wasn't up for knighting, or for receiving the Order of The British Empire. Then as mentioned in the last chapter, my research led me to the Queen's annual Garden Parties. Once I got up to speed on what these are I had found my *specific objective*: try somehow to get myself invited to one of the Garden Parties.

Just as you saw earlier in this chapter, once an objective is specific enough, the right questions can be formulated to inch you closer and closer to meeting the objective. Having a clear objective also focuses your efforts. For the past eight months now I have kept that one goal central in everything I do.

It is now only a matter of weeks for me to find out if everything I have done and described in this book will garner for me one of the highly sought after invitations to a Garden Party.

Chapter 9

PREPARATION – DO YOUR HOMEWORK

There Are No Shortcuts

Next up in our preparation is the imperative of doing your homework. Sorry, I did not warn you – did you hear a voice in your head from your childhood blaring at you? Well, just because we're no longer in primary school doesn't mean that homework is not important.

Speaking of school, when I was in grad school years ago I discovered an unpleasant fact – my thesis supervisor was known for keeping his grad students for two to three years at the masters' level. Now in Canada, that's a bit long as many students want to move on to do PhDs and complete these before they hit middle age. If I had done my homework by asking a few simple questions of my supervisor's other students before signing on I would have spared myself the surprise. A little homework can pay big dividends.

Well, we probably can all confess to not having done our homework at least once. An excuse I hear often from children is that they did not know that an assignment was due or worse, that they weren't aware that there was any homework assigned at all. As most parents know, these are indefensible positions! For us, in learning to observe better, basic homework is usually pretty obvious. Take the different professional question-askers that we are gleaning principles from for example.

Family doctors are expected to read up on a patient's medical history before rushing into diagnosis. Patients also count on doctors to keep up-to-date on the latest clinical advances and treatments. When you are sitting in a doctor's examining room waiting for your turn, do you ever look at all those framed credentials on the wall? Beyond the fancy calligraphy and titles I always look for one thing – the date. When did the doctor last spend time learning something new? You can check out doctors online but usually these sources only disclose where a doctor graduated from and whether there are any complaints.

My first family doctor in childhood was a kind and patient physician but over the decades I had my doubts whether he continued to do his homework. Apparently towards the end of his career, he would respond to a patient's complaint about, say swollen finger joints by thrusting his own swollen fingers in front of the patient explaining "You think that's bad, look at my fingers". So pay attention to those framed documents next time.

Media interviewers that line up interesting guest personalities also have obvious homework to prepare. It is true that sometimes actors are paid to host interview programs so the real grunt work is done by unnamed researchers toiling in the background, but someone on the team needs to read up on the personality to formulate some engaging questions.

Frost vs. Nixon

Sir David Frost, the legendary Emmy Award-winning British interviewer, producer, and publisher, knew how important doing his homework would be before doing interviews. Mr. Frost is probably best known for the revelatory interviews he conducted with former US President Richard Nixon in 1977.

Mr. Nixon was facing impeachment over the Watergate scandal. In 1972 during his re-election campaign, there was a botched break-in at the Democratic National Committee offices in the Watergate office and apartment complex in Washington D.C. The break-in was executed to repair a telephone bugging device. The subsequent investigations determined that the bugging and the break-in were directed by senior White House staff and that the White House later initiated a cover-up. President Nixon was almost impeached by the US Congress and convicted by the US Senate for his role in the cover-up, avoiding impeachment and conviction only by resigning office in 1974. Mr. Nixon became the only US president to date to ever end his term through resignation.

Mr. Frost recounts in his book *Frost/Nixon: Behind The Scenes Of The Nixon Interviews*, the extraordinary events leading up to his historic multi-session interview of Mr. Nixon in 1977. The edited interviews were broadcast and in 2008, Ron Howard directed a film, *Frost/Nixon*, dramatizing these events.

The astounding admission that Mr. Frost extracted out of Mr. Nixon during the interviews had its beginnings in the intense and thorough homework done over several months by Mr. Frost's principal researcher, Jim Reston. Mr. Reston dug out from among the Watergate trial prosecution exhibits audio-taped conversations of Mr. Nixon admitting that he was well aware of the cover-up attempts (like other presidents, Mr. Nixon had tape recording equipment installed in the White House).

One of the condemning taped sound bites was the following (Mr. Nixon was speaking): "When I'm speaking about Watergate, that's the whole point of the election: this tremendous investigation rests unless one of the seven [accused in the affair] begins to talk: that's the problem" (Frost 18). In other words, Mr. Nixon seemed to be quite aware that the indictment against him would succeed or fail based on whether any of the accused White House staffers chose to betray the President. As we will see in the chapter, *Technique - Soften Up Your Audience*, Mr. Frost built on this evidence to later bring Mr. Nixon to acknowledge that he knew about the cover-up earlier than he had ever previously admitted (which means he could have done something about it, but to his shame, did not).

A good number of highly motivated congressmen, senators, and special prosecutors had all failed to bring an admission of guilt from Mr. Nixon. Watergate had cast a pallor over the US and the prevailing sentiment in America was one of justice denied. Only Mr. Frost was able to draw out Mr. Nixon's unexpected admission that would help to bring some closure to the nation's cynicism. There are many lessons to be learned from the Frost/Nixon interviews that will improve your questioning ability, but the big takeaway in this first chapter on the importance of preparation is that good old fashioned homework will lay the foundation for getting results.

Now, to keep things in perspective, not all of the homework principles will require you to sequester yourself for months to do research like Mr. Frost and his team. Suppose you are buying a home. There is obvious homework like choosing a realtor, doing a home inspection, and arranging financing. But if you really want to know if you should buy, you should do a little sleuthing. Drive by the property in the daytime and in the evening to see the traffic patterns. Visit the local school at dismissal time to see what kind of people live in the neighbourhood. Talk to the letter carrier (who else goes up to every house in the neighbourhood and knows more about your potential neighbours?).

The Business Of Homework

In the area of sales, I have discovered that one the most productive homework exercises is to find the "org chart" (organization chart) that describes the "who's who" of your customer or partner team. Earlier I had mentioned LinkedIn as a treasure trove of information about people and how they are connected. That old saying "It's not what you know but who you know" is timeless.

If you are selling, you know you need to find out who needs your product or service and who has to approve the purchase. This is not nearly as simple as it sounds. From my experience selling software to big banks, you may find yourself in front of a governance board, an architecture standards board, an applications team, an infrastructure engineering group, and the support and operations committee. And this is at one bank for one sale. Sometimes I think it would be simpler to deal with the United Nations!

But if you are going to succeed in dealing with large organizations, you need that org chart. Then when one group tries to stall, you can leverage another group to get things moving again. You can build support by knowing who is in charge and how each of these groups work together (or do not work together). Now I know why heads of state have such large entourages to "work the back room".

Also, being able to throw some names around from the org chart at the opportune moment can be indispensable in keeping momentum going in your discussions. Just try to arrange a meeting with a senior executive – unless you can credibly drop some names from the org chart, the executive's administrator will block your progress every time.

Now how to get that org chart is another exercise in asking good questions. You can ask straight out for it, and once in a blue moon I've actually received one, so do not be afraid to ask that most basic question. However, things are seldom so easy. You can make up your own org chart by asking people some basic questions like "To whom do you report?" or "How many people are on your team?" - these questions almost always work.

And as mentioned in an earlier chapter, *Attitude – Be Thorough*, I would never *only* ask these questions, I would then immediately ask for the *title* of a person's manager. With a title you can size up the importance of the person (though beware of inflated titles – for example in most banks, it seems like everyone is a Vice-President). More significantly, with individual title information, you can figure out department titles and then when you are talking to someone else in that company, you can make reference to the department. This all builds credibility because you are now talking the language of the company. With each passing person you speak to from the company, you then ask that person where they fit in your org chart and pretty soon you'll have a working copy. This is the power of doing your homework.

Doing Your Homework And The Queen

I must admit that when I embarked on my quest to try to meet the Queen I was faced with my first challenge: I knew very little about Her Majesty. What little I knew came more from the media (which seems to have a love-hate relationship with the royal family) and from watching the Hollywood film, *The Queen* (starring Helen Mirren, who won the Best Actress Oscar in 2007 for her portrayal of the Queen).

Preparation – Do Your Homework   113

So off to my local public library I went to start a reading binge on all things royal. I read about Her Majesty's parents (King George VI and Queen Elizabeth, who later was known as the Queen Mother). I read about the early years of the Queen and her sister, Princess Margaret. I read about the Queen's romance with Prince Philip. I read about the Queen's succession to the throne and about her personal likes, dislikes, habits, and values. I read about how the Queen's agenda and affairs are managed. All the while I kept one question in my mind – "What is the best approach in order to try to meet with the Queen?"

At the time of my initial research I had no clue as to what that approach would look like. But by maintaining the right attitudes – curiosity, creativity, thoroughness, persistence, and skepticism I kept at it. As mentioned in the earlier chapter, *Attitude – Be Skeptical*, I had a breakthrough when I learned of the Queen's annual Garden Parties. This was the result of doing some online homework – I found the official website for the British monarchy:

http://www.royal.gov.uk/HMTheQueen/ContactTheQueen/Overview.aspx

From all of these book and online sources, I began to develop my opinions about the royal family, some positive, some less so. I started to learn some insider lingo, how to address the Queen (e.g. as "Her Majesty"), and also to put together a kind of org chart of key people and how they are related (e.g. the Lord Chamberlain, the Ladies-in-Waiting, the Secretary to the Queen).

I'll provide more details in the next chapter, *Preparation – Know Your Audience* but I'll share one of the outcomes of my homework now. In one of my research books I discovered that the Queen has a department in the Buckingham Palace org chart named the Palace Information Office. I even saw a photo of that office in one of my sources, which went further to disclose that there is a palace staffer in that Office who handles the Queen's correspondence. Well, given that I had sent a package to Her Majesty I was keenly interested in whether the package would ever make its way to the Queen. By doing my homework, I was rewarded with the name of this key individual in the Palace's inner workings – her name is Jane Smith. Right. Perhaps she's related to the ubiquitous "Jane Doe"! Good, you're learning some healthy skepticism.

Not so fast. A research source clarified that *"Jane Smith"* is indeed a pseudonym, i.e. not her real name. But even with a pseudonym in an org chart, this had to be useful. I picked up the phone and called Buckingham Palace. Did I get through? You'll have to read on. Suffice it to say … do your homework.

Chapter 10

PREPARATION – KNOW YOUR AUDIENCE

Comedians – Masters Of Observation

A distinct part of doing your homework is to know your audience – the recipient of your questions. This makes particular sense for those vocations that directly involve interviewing others. Of course the audience goes by different names in each vocation: media interviewers have *guests*, doctors have *patients*, lawyers have *witnesses*, investigators have *suspects*. But in each instance, if you do not know enough about your audience, you may as well just refer to them as blocks of wood because you will be in for a lot of silence.

Comedian Bob Newhart confides in his book, *I Shouldn't Even Be Doing This!*, that those in the comedy business are painfully aware of this principle. Mr. Newhart recounts the first time he hosted the iconic live comedy show, *Saturday Night Live*. One sketch saw Mr. Newhart dressed like a Union soldier during the US Civil War. He was supposed to write a condolence letter for a soldier who had died, but he kept forgetting to write. Throughout the sketch, common objects and tasks remind the soldier repeatedly that he has to write the letter.

Now, if you've never seen or heard Mr. Newhart you should. His trademark low key delivery adds punch to his punch-lines. However, that night the routine received no laughter because Mr. Newhart did not know his audience (175-176). Just the evening before, the US military had failed to rescue fifty-two American hostages held in Iran for over a year, losing two aircraft and several lives in the process ("Iran Hostage Crisis").

If we can learn from stand-up comics, we can also learn from comic strips. Regular Dilbert readers know that the author, Scott Adams, lampoons engineers. I have visited technology companies whose offices routinely sport a Dilbert strip in some cubicle because Mr. Adams understands his audience. According to *Wikipedia*, Mr. Adams came by his insights honestly: he was himself a computer programmer early on in his career ("Scott Adams").

Keep Tabs On Your Audience

To know your audience, you have to do some groundwork. Collecting information to build a personal profile requires a combination of initial research and then ongoing refinement as you learn more. Let me emphasize the *learning* aspects otherwise you'll be stymied in the classic "chicken and egg" standoff. That's because the aim of knowing your audience is to enable you to ask better questions, but you need to ask questions in the first place to know your audience.

I do not have the best memory so I've always compensated by being a compulsive documenter. When I meet someone for the first time I usually create a contact in my smartphone's address book, including facts that will help me to remember the person. If the name is unusual (e.g. Agueda) I will write out the name phonetically (e.g. "Ag-way-da"). Typically, I will add some details on the person's appearance, most often by choosing a TV or film actor who bears some resemblance – this way when I meet the person the second time, I will be better equipped to recall (and pronounce) the person's name correctly – these minor details open the way for your audience to respond more warmly and more comprehensively to your questions.

Following face/name recognition, I will ask unthreatening questions and record the responses in my address book to form a snapshot of this person. For example, I might ask about where a person resides ("Do you live near the office?") or if I walk by the person's desk and I see photos I will ask about the subjects. It is important to be curious, but at the same time not to pry.

Once I was having dinner with a product marketing manager at a trade show in Mountain View, California. He was having wine with his meal so I casually asked him to tell me his favourite wine. I recorded this seemingly unimportant fact. Less than a year later he ended up leaving his company. He had been a great business partner so I had a gift sent to his home - a case of wine - his *favourite* wine. Within a year he contacted me and we ended up doing business again on an important and lucrative project. This is not to say that the wine sealed the deal, but asking little questions to know your audience better can take you places.

Head Games

In *How To Interview – The Art of the Media Interview,* author Paul McLaughlin quotes Terence McKenna, then a journalist with the CBC's TV news program, *The Journal*: "I approach these confrontational or aggressive interviews a lot like a chess game, planning them out a great deal. The first thing I do is make a list of questions. Then I try to really put myself in their skin and think how they will answer. So I would block an interview out, saying, if I ask this question they will likely say that, in which case I can come to a follow-up question ... You really try to think of *how they think* [italics added], of what their answers will be" (McLaughlin 123).

The chess game comparison was drawn in the earlier chapter, *Attitude – Be Thorough*, but it is an apt comparison here also. In effect, to know your audience better, you are trying to develop some empathy, some connection, some understanding of how your audience thinks and responds.

As a simple example, take the case of a parent asking a child whether the homework is done yet. A common but poor question would be "Did you finish your homework?" Many parents will tell you that the answer is often affirmative but nothing could be further from the truth. Sage parents (aka parents who have been burned in the past) will ask a better question: "Can you show me your homework now?" The difference comes from having experience, knowing how children tend to respond. And that shapes a better question.

Here's another favourite of mine, which takes the case of that same child who has now blossomed into a teen. Now teens are constantly asking for money, i.e. for an "allowance". I like to ask parents if they give their children this "freebie". Sometimes parents proudly respond that they are shrewder than that, that they only dole out cash when their teens do some household chore, like washing the dishes or taking out the garbage. Now don't get me wrong, that's progressive, it's on the right track. You may not agree with me but in my parenting philosophy, children should pull their own weight in the home because that is what family is all about. So children should not be paid for doing what they should be doing in the first place. And allowance? I'm paying for their food, clothes, supplies, medical, entertainment, vacations, tuition, living expenses – so excuse me, what is the allowance for? There are part-time jobs for that extra cash they need.

While this draconian philosophy is well known in my home, that does not mean that the petition for allowance or payment for chores is ignored outright. Since I know my audience and fully anticipate these requests, I do not push back, nor do I launch into a long lecture. Quite the opposite. I calmly ask "How much do you want?" followed by a commensurate request for repayment for food consumed, rent, bus fare, ... you get the picture. After all, if the argument is "to be fair", then I think *that* is very fair – payment for services rendered for *all* parties, not just them. My teens laugh at this point because they know the drill and honestly, they understand the logic.

Hockey Games

Back in the boom days of the Internet (1999-2000) I was heading business development for a software company partnered with Sun Microsystems Inc. (now part of Oracle Corp.). At the time, Sun's long time irrepressible CEO, Scott McNealy, was a mover and shaker in the industry. To put our company on the map I had a plan to invite Mr. McNealy to Toronto.

But why would Sun's CEO leave the sunny climes of corporate headquarters in Silicon Valley to meet a fledgling partner in the "great white north"? Audience research provided the answer.

It turns out that the Californian CEO loved to play ice hockey (he was born and raised in the US Midwest). I had plans to rent iconic *Maple Leaf Gardens* where the National Hockey League Toronto Maple Leafs once played and to invite Mr. McNealy for a little game of pickup hockey. Of course during and after the game would be plenty of time for questions that could increase our partner standing.

Then the dot-com crash came. Before I could send the invitation the tech bubble deflated. Sun's fortunes declined beyond the reach of a shinny game. However, the point remains: know your audience.

Know Thy Opponent

Earlier we had drawn some principles from the Frost/Nixon interviews. Bob Zelnick was a key member of Mr. Frost's team. Mr. Zelnick is a seasoned reporter and former National Public Radio (NPR) Bureau Chief. He applied this principle of knowing your audience well.

At one point in the run-up to the Nixon interviews, Mr. Zelnick sensed that Mr. Frost was not taking the preparation seriously enough, so Mr. Zelnick chided Mr. Frost: "Don't you know what you're up against? This man [Mr. Nixon] is not only one of America's cagiest politicians, he's been a member of the bar [i.e. a lawyer] for almost forty years … by [the time of the next interview session] he will have committed every word on every Watergate tape to memory. He'll know every statue cold … You're in against a master, man, a master. … And he's a fighter" (95). History shows that Mr. Frost and his team took this exhortation to heart. They redoubled their efforts to prepare, producing Mr. Nixon's candid admissions referred to previously in this book.

Go Deeper

From the medical field come more insights. In *Talking With Patients About Spirituality and Worldview*, we read that "Religious and spiritual questioning during an interview can improve a treatment alliance, because patients feel that important aspects of their existence are understood" (Josephson, and Peteet 182). Asking about a patient's spirituality in an initial diagnostic interview can be a minefield but it can also yield positive results. Getting to the heart of a patient's concerns improves patient care and deepens the clinician's understanding of the patient" (Josephson, and Peteet 195).

Here are some sample questions that some clinicians use to help them know their patients better:

- "Is religious faith an important, daily part of your life?"

- "How has this faith influenced your life?"

- "Are you currently part of a religious community?"

- "Are there spiritual aspects that you would like to address in the development of a treatment plan?"

(Josephson, and Peteet 187)

Knowing Your Audience And The Queen

Like most celebrities, the royal family is careful to guard its privacy. There is a British Monarchy Facebook page and a similar Twitter account, but these are not personally frequented by Her Majesty.

So as I turned to good old-fashioned books to compose my own profile of the Queen, I found some facts that I recorded (**bold face** marks the facts that I made direct use of in my quest to meet the Queen):

TABLE 10-1 A Profile of the Queen

Profile	Details
Personal Values	She is considerate, efficient, **dutiful [I used the "call to duty" to help people observe better as the motive for writing this book, which I referred to in my letter]**, and private. She values courage, decency, duty, sagacity, courtesy, reasonableness (Nicholson 36).
Likes	She loves order, punctuality, and **decorum [I made sure to use all the royal titles like "Your Majesty", "His Royal Highness"]** (Nicholson 25), (Davies 262).
Dislikes	She doesn't enjoy intellectual talk, opera, ballet, classical concerts. She rarely reads books (Nicholson 38).
Nuances	She is ambivalent about faith but attends **church [I disclosed how some of my church friends had met her or one of the royal family]** dutifully (Nicholson 39, 128).
Personality	She is strong-minded, intelligent, a straight shooter. She never shows off, is pleasant but not comic, **she doesn't joke [so I kept my tone serious with deference]**. Her natural instinct is to play things safe (Nicholson 52, 68, 127).
Challenges	She is not good handling unfamiliar situations (Nicholson 19, 116).
Tastes	She eats simply. She thinks that caviar, foie gras, and champagne are a waste of money. She is particular about her food presentation though – food must be

Profile	Details
	cut to the same size. She takes her tea with cold milk, no sugar; she occasionally eats her favourite – **Dundee cake [well, I did consider sending her some of this traditional Scottish fruit cake, but I thought the Dick Francis novel would travel better!]** (Davies 263, 271). Her favourite cocktail is "The Zara", red Dubonnet and gin with a twist of lemon that she likes to enjoy before lunch; she allegedly picked up this preference from her mother (Sismondo).
Practices	After every gathering she "insists that every letter of thanks arriving at the palace be **read personally by her [this tidbit gave me hope that the Queen might actually personally read my letter – hence all the horse-themed images and the book I enclosed]**; she is very mindful of anyone who does NOT thank her after an event. "Each day Elizabeth spends at least an hour discussing her future diary with her Private Secretary ..." (Davies 265, 270).

Profile	Details
Interests	She sometimes reads Sporting Life or reads about her favourite subject – horse breeding, after lunch. "She still hopes to put together a combination that will achieve her greatest ambition, to win the English Derby". She enjoys watching comedy shows and some old films; she enjoys movies. She doesn't read as much now but executives at Hatchards, the booksellers in Piccadilly, send current titles to her; she prefers biographies, thrillers, award-winning novels, and especially likes **Dick Francis [you know already I sent his then latest novel to her]**, since his thrillers revolve around horse racing. She loves after-dinner games like charades (Davies 269, 276, 279).

After all this research I would hardly consider myself an expert, or even a "royal watcher". You couldn't pin any paparazzi label on me. Besides, we in Canada are known for being low key. Alas, I know the Queen a so much better now, even if still only from afar.

Chapter 11

PREPARATION – CHOOSE THE RIGHT PERSON

Finding Mr. Right

I said it earlier and I'll say it again: "It's not what you know but whom you know". But equally important, you have to know that whom you know, knows what you want to know! In other words, after all your hard work in getting your attitude right and your preparation done, do not squander it by then asking your questions to the *wrong* person.

Children instinctively understand this principle – if they need money, or permission to have a sleepover, or a signature on a sub-par math test, they know which parent to ask. Adults on the other hand are not always up to the task.

In the sales profession, getting to the right person (at the right time) is a survival skill. I've had sales people tell me that their deal would close imminently. How do they know? They would explain that their purchase order is being processed by the purchasing department. True as that may be, often this is as un-bankable as "the cheque is in the mail" refrain. When I pressed for more assurance, the sales people would dutifully ring up the purchasing agent, who would reiterate that the order is being processed. And so the merry-go-round keeps spinning around.

The best person, the *right* person to push for clarity is not a minion in purchasing or accounting - it's the person with the *money*. Follow up should always be with the customer from the line of business who will use the solution and who will be paying the bill.

Finding Mr. Wrong

Just to demonstrate that I am still learning all the APT principles along with you, I remember being on vacation in Florida, the destination of choice for us snow-bound Canadians. On the drive back north from Orlando we decided to do a little exploring in Daytona Beach. If you know the area, it has long stretches of Atlantic Ocean-front beach, a famous NASCAR raceway, and that balmy warm weather that we were in no hurry to trade for snow and slush.

The only problem was we couldn't find the beach. They call the city Daytona *Beach*. But for the life of me, there was no beach to be found. With pride in check (or in tatters) I pulled the car over on a major street and asked a pedestrian for directions. Turns out he was not very accurate as his directions were wrong. My travelling companions were doubled over in laughter because I had picked a random guy on the street who was next seen pushing an empty grocery cart down the middle of the road. In retrospect he was likely a homeless person - not the right person to ask directions of. You can be creative, persistent, thorough ... but if you ask the wrong person, you get the wrong answer (we eventually did find the beach and it was worth the humiliation).

The Better Half

By the way, how was it that I ended up on vacation in the first place? I, like thousands of unwitting others, had purchased a vacation timeshare. If you've ever been to places like Orlando and Las Vegas – highly valued getaway locations – you have probably been offered sizeable discounts on tickets to Disney World or a Blue Man Group show. All you had to do in exchange was attend a two hour sales presentation over breakfast or lunch.

Let's see, two tickets to a Disney theme park might set you back close to two hundred dollars so any discount is a big deal. But if you pay attention, they always have a stipulation when you sign up for the presentation. The sales people insist that if you are married, both husband and wife must attend. Why? I think a big reason is that these professionals know who the right person is to ask for a purchase decision.

When we went to our first ever presentation I steeled myself to say "no". I figured they were giving away free prizes so what was the worst that could happen? I forgot about my "better half". As the math and numbers guy in the relationship I was doing the computations but the sales people gave up on me and went to work on my wife. "What is your dream vacation?" they plied. Then out would come these sensational picture books of Hawaii and other exotic destinations.

We were sunk. The timeshare sales person knew the principle, "Ask the right person, get the right answer".

Cruise You Lose

So how are you supposed to find this "right person" (or persons – more likely there will be many people)? Let me suggest at least one "algorithm" using the APT Principles we have covered so far. We'll make up a scenario – say you are trying to pick the best cruise ship line for your young family to take a summer voyage to the Caribbean:

TABLE 11-1 Finding The Right Person For Cruise Advice

APT Principle	Choosing the Right Person to Ask
Have a Specific Objective	To narrow down your objective, you have to decide what "best cruise ship" means. It could be lowest cost, most interesting ports of call, highest food quality, best entertainment, top safety record etc. I will guess that for most people, "best cruise ship" means best passenger experience, meaning most on-board fun. So the objective is to ask questions to determine which cruise ship is the most fun.
Do Your Homework	You can do a lot of research up front and online. What activities are offered? Do they have supervised activities for children of all ages? Are there family-oriented events? What amenities are there? Do they have a video game arcade? A splash pool? An ice skating rink? A surfing simulator?

APT Principle	Choosing the Right Person to Ask
	In the end, you need to be a bit skeptical (are you going to believe everything the cruise line marketing department pumps out?), so next you have to start asking questions of people you know to get to the right person.
Know Your Audience	So like LinkedIn, start with someone in your closest circle of contacts who has been on a cruise. If there's no one in that category, pick someone you know who knows someone who's gone on a cruise, or has ever researched going on a cruise.

If there is absolutely no one even fitting that description you might need to cold call the cruise line directly. Just do not give them your credit card number on first blush.

Ask the curious questions below of your audience based on how much actual experience they have in cruising, and expect that you'll have to talk to a chain of people – as you get answers to your curious questions, you'll come up with new questions, and you'll be referred to other people ... i.e. you'll be getting closer and closer to the right person. |
| Be Curious | Like we learned from Leonardo Da Vinci, take notes because you'll probably be asking questions of multiple people. Especially jot down your W5+H (who, what, where, when, why, how) questions like:
- Who looks after children's programs (i.e. are they baby sitters or trained in early |

APT Principle	Choosing the Right Person to Ask
	childhood studies)? - What is there to do on the ship on the days in port if you choose to stay onboard? - Where are the different activities on the ship in relation to where your cabin might be? - When do all the fun attractions start and stop each day? - Why can we not change our dining options from day-to-day rather than locking into formal dining or something else? - How much do the "extras" cost (e.g. shore excursions, "premium" restaurants, spa sessions etc.)?
Be Persistent	As I said, there will be a whole chain of people you'll end up asking your questions to, and each one will probably lead you closer and closer to an "expert" who can answer your curious questions, address your skepticism, and challenge your assumptions. You can also expect that you will not get to this "expert" the first time you start asking questions. Do not give up!

Back To Six

Finding the right person is critical to getting quality answers to your questions. Dating websites use a battery of questions about your likes, dislikes, background, hobbies, habits, expectations, and values to try to match you with that right person. I admit to having done some research on dating websites once (in preparation for a speaking engagement, not a wedding engagement) and was appalled that questions on values were so scarce. It seems that "what movies you like to watch" can be ranked as importantly as your views on faith. Scary.

I think a better model for finding the right person to address your questions is the good old "six degrees of separation" theory that I made reference to earlier in the book. As you start probing your network of contacts with your questions to ultimately satisfy your specific objective, you will probably end up dealing with up to six people before you get your questions answered. This is not a scientific theory, just an empirical guess. If you end up having to work through *more than six* people then you really have learned to be persistent, and that's a good skill to have, as long as it does not turn into nagging!

Choose The Right Person And The Queen

You already know that in the spirit of "doing my homework" I had read broadly about the royal family and had been sending off emails, making calls, and of course, mailing my special package directly to the Queen.

As I think back over the chain of people that I had to work through it looks like this:

TABLE 11-2 Sequence of Events Contacting the Queen

Sequence (& Date)	Outcome
1 (April 14)	First decided to try to meet with the Queen.

Began reserving books about the royal family from my public library for research.

Checked out LinkedIn and Facebook to try to find someone I knew who could connect me to the Queen – none existed. |
| 2 (April 27) | Books received from the library. Started reading and learned that Buckingham Palace has a Palace Information Office with a woman with the pseudonym, "Jane Smith" handling the Queen's correspondence. This could be the "right person" to ask my questions to! (Hardman 24) |
| 3 (May 16) | **Contact: Buckingham Palace Operator (London)**

Called the Palace for the very first time. So unreal to be speaking to someone there, even just the Palace Operator.

I asked to be put through to the Palace Information Office. The Operator asked for the nature of inquiry and I lost my nerve and simply asked this question: "I would like to send a book to Her Majesty – could you please confirm the mailing address?"

It was confirmed as:

Buckingham Palace
London SW1A 1AA |

Preparation – Choose The Right Person 133

Sequence (& Date)	Outcome
4 (May 16)	**Contact: Office of the Governor General of Canada (Rideau Hall, Ottawa)** While I was working out a second approach to the Palace, I called and asked if there were any upcoming royal visits to Canada. My objective changed to trying to find an alternative venue for meeting the Queen in case I bombed out with the Palace. I was passed off to Canadian Heritage, a Canadian federal government agency.
5 (May 16)	**Contact: Canadian Heritage (Ottawa)** I asked my question again about potential royal visits to Canada. I was told there were no upcoming visits by the Queen. HRH Prince William and his soon-to-be new wife Catherine (Kate), the next Duchess of Cambridge, would be visiting Canada later in the year. I decided to get some independent verification that the Queen's Garden Parties were real. I asked for confirmation of the protocol for getting invited. Instead of getting an answer to my question, I was sent back to the Governor General. Now I knew I was dealing with a government agency!
6 (May 17)	Well, I had at least received confirmation from Buckingham Palace as to their mailing address, so I mailed off my package to the Queen by regular post.

Sequence (& Date)	Outcome
7 (May 19)	**Contact: Office of the Governor General of Canada (Rideau Hall, Ottawa)** You may have detected that I do not like to rely on one "Right Person", or to do things in sequence – it is always better to keep momentum going, however small, by having *multiple* questions going to *multiple* potential "Right Persons". Since Heritage Canada sent me back to the Governor General, I changed the mode of communication, sending an email this time instead of phoning. I asked for clarification and information on the Garden Parties. In applying the attitudes of being *skeptical* and *creative*, I anticipated that I might not get very far so I included in my email that I had a (tenuous) connection to the Governor General (we both have roots in the same university – okay, I was only a lowly alumnus while he had been its President, but still I had to try). I'm not sure all that got me any further as I was then referred to the High Commission of Canada in London. I was starting to feel passed around ... but that's why the attitude of *persistence* is important!

Sequence (& Date)	Outcome
8 (May 23 – 27)	**Contact: High Commission of Canada (London)** I sent an email to the High Commission's Royal Events Co-ordinator and finally got all the details on the protocol for the Garden Parties. You never waste an opportunity to probe, so I asked additional questions to learn more about the invitation process. From the High Commission's responses to my extra questions, I then understood what the application process entailed and what my odds of success were.
9 (June 9)	**Contact: Buckingham Palace** I decided it was time to try Buckingham Palace again. This time when the Palace Operator said in the same crisp British accent as last time "Buckingham Palace – How may I direct your call?" I asked straight away for Jane Smith of the Palace Information Office. There was a noticeable delay (and a long holding of breath) but then I was put through! Since there was a Canadian postal strike of all things in progress during this time, I explained that I had sent a book to the Queen and then I asked "Jane Smith" this question: "How long does it take for a response, and would it be by mail as we have a mail strike in Canada".

Sequence (& Date)	Outcome
9 (June 9) cont'd.	I was hoping for some escalation due to the unusual circumstances with the strike. However, "Jane Smith" responded "The backlog is more than three weeks now, normally there is a two to three week response; however, with the royal wedding [HRH Prince William & HRH Catherine, future Duchess of Cambridge] there was a larger backlog than normal". Well, being a "mathie", I figured then that I was in for a long wait (using the attitudes of *being thorough* and *being skeptical*). I sent the package May 17 and called "Jane Smith" June 9, making that three weeks, two days. If a response normally took two to three weeks, but was backlogged by three weeks, then I would not have a response for five to six weeks (meaning between June 21 to 28). Again in order to be *thorough*, I did not waste the opportunity of speaking to the Queen's head of correspondence – I asked about the Garden Parties, and then in a great twist of humour, "Jane Smith" thought for a moment then said "You're from Canada … do you know a David Johnston?" Very funny "Jane" … I do know (of) David Johnston, aka the Governor General of Canada. Round and round we go …

Sequence (& Date)	Outcome
10 (June 29)	**Contact: Lady Susan Hussey (Lady-in-Waiting, Woman of the Bedchamber) – (London)** Well, I did indeed receive a response letter from the Queen's senior Lady-in-Waiting, Lady Susan Hussey. This was astounding enough because this meant that my package was positively received by "Jane Smith", and because the response did not come from Jane or someone reporting to her, I believe it meant that my package was deemed important enough to be sent to the Queen and for her to dispatch a response through her senior Lady-in-Waiting! But what was even more astounding was the date on the letter and the date on the postmarked letter (see below for images) from Buckingham Palace – June 10. Remember, I had spoken to "Jane Smith" on June 9 and told to expect a response two to three weeks later. So how did my package garner a response *the very next day?*. Maybe I'm being too optimistic, but I think there's a plausible case here that my package got expedited through the Queen's office due to my call. Did I in the end find the "Right Person" – indeed, I believe I did!

And one more unusual detail. I had mentioned that little theory that it generally takes up to six people before you can find the "Right

Person". Over the two and a half months that my little odyssey above took to play out, I had talked to a number of people, while getting passed (expectedly) from person to person.

Here's the cast in chronological order by first appearance in the story:
1. Buckingham Palace Operator
2. Governor General's inquiries staff
3. Canadian Heritage inquiries staff
4. High Commission, Royal Events Co-ordinator
5. "Jane Smith", Palace Information Office
6. Lady Susan Hussey, Woman of the Bedchamber

Exactly SIX. Persistence pays off to get to the Right Person.

FIGURE 11-1 Buckingham Palace's Response Letter To The Author (note the date: June 10, 2011, one day after the author spoke to "Jane Smith")

BUCKINGHAM PALACE

10th June, 2011

Dear Mr. Lee,

The Queen wishes me to write and thank you for your letter, the photograph, and the present of the book which you have sent.

It was kind of you to send the delightful picture of your niece presenting flowers to Her Majesty in Toronto, and The Queen was pleased to be reminded of this happy visit she made with The Duke of Edinburgh in 2002.

In your letter you say that you are writing a book which you would like to present to The Queen at a later date, and I have to explain that although Her Majesty would like to be able to see the many people who ask to meet her when they visit this country, I am afraid that because of the number of official engagements and public audiences, it is sadly impossible for her to do so.

I think you would like to know that if you and your wife wish to apply to attend a Royal Garden Party then you should write to the Canadian High Commission in London, MacDonald House, 1 Grosvenor Square, London W1K 4AB, who may be able to assist, as these Garden Parties can be attended by sponsored invitation only.

I am to thank you once again for your thoughtful gift, and for your message of good wishes which The Queen greatly appreciated.

Yours Sincerely,

Susan Hussey

Lady-in-Waiting

Mr A Lee

Chapter 12

PREPARATION – DON'T ASSUME

Analyze That

You have now made it to the final chapter on preparation. This principle is cast in the negative, that is, something we must *not* do in our preparation - that is we must not make assumptions.

Going back to the software startup I had co-founded, I remember the very first research analyst briefing I ever participated in. In many industries, market research analysts offer their clients insights into market trends, performance metrics, and key and emerging industry players. These insights come at a hefty price, costing tens of thousands of dollars annually. Nonetheless, an analyst's clients rely on this data to make decisions for procurement, product research, competitive positioning etc.

And startups depend on analysts to cover them in their reports so that potential customers and partners will embrace them. So with all that in mind, I contacted one of the most senior database analysts at Gartner, the number one information technology analyst firm, and arranged to give a briefing on our company.

For a first briefing the call seemed to go well. So well that I ventured to ask the analyst if he intended to ink some words about us. I received a resounding "no". Reading between the lines and the tone of the analyst's voice, I inferred that what he was saying was "Are you kidding? That's not how the game is played."

I had naively assumed that merely speaking to an analyst would result in research coverage. Bad assumption.

Leave No Stone

We met Mike Wallace a few chapters earlier – Mr. Wallace was the storied interviewer and mainstay of the CBS news program, *60 Minutes*. One of Mr. Wallace's interviews was with the famed US architect, Frank Lloyd Wright, designer of over five hundred buildings including the Guggenheim Museum in New York City ("Frank Lloyd Wright"):

> [Mr. Wright] ... it's so unbecoming to say [that he is the greatest architect of the twentieth century] ... I'm not as crude, as arrogant, as I'm generally reported to be.
>
> [Mr. Wallace] What is arrogance?
>
> [Mr. Wright] Arrogance is something a man possesses on the surface, to defend the fact that he hasn't got the things he pretends to have. (Wallace 138).

I do not know about you but I think that's a pretty insightful definition of arrogance. The point is that Mr. Wallace did not make any assumptions – when his guest used the word "arrogance", Mr. Wallace pressed for a definition.

I am going to make an assumption that we've all made assumptions. Every time I walk upon an argument in progress between my kids I certainly jump to assume who is right and who is wrong.

Who's The Terrorist?

In *I Can Read You Like A Book*, author Gregory Hartley, a former US Army Intelligence Officer and Trainer, discloses some of the secrets of his trade. Mr. Hartley trains his clients to read body language and verbal responses to discern the truth. In a training simulation to identify a supposed terrorist, Mr. Hartley introduces us to a group of five people (three men, two women) who are having dinner in a farmhouse.

One of the three men has a prominent scar and the investigator in the exercise asks what this man's occupation is – the man responds that he sells "timers and radios". Based on this disclosure, you might immediately conclude (i.e. assume) you have found the terrorist.

However, the second man in the room speaks up, trying to draw suspicion away from the scarred man, identifying himself as an electronics repairman. Hmm, timers and radios vs. electronics ... all of these could be components for producing or setting off explosives. So now is the repairman the terrorist?

The repairman's wife spits at the investigator – she clearly despises westerners, but does that single her out?

The third man, the repairman's brother, owns the farmhouse and is a sheep farmer. This man's wife is also present. She answers some seemingly basic informational questions showing her to be more educated than the others.

The investigator chooses to zoom in on the repairman's wife, the woman with the strong negative attitude towards westerners, but only so that he can observe how the *others* in the room respond. She succumbs by pointing to the educated woman, screaming that that woman has the most anti-western sentiments. The educated woman counters by striding confidently up to the investigator and telling him face-to-face that her sentiments are based on her first-hand witnessing of war violence.

Which one is the terrorist?

The first assumption would be that the terrorist is a man, perhaps the repairman in particular, since he would have facility with devices that could be made into roadside bombs. However, Mr. Hartley explains that there are clear signs that the *educated woman* is the suspect because she had been pointed out by the other woman, and because she behaves like she has had more exposure to western culture. The scenario concludes with the explanation that the educated woman indeed has contacts in Western Europe which enables her to access bomb-making expertise and material to bring home for terrorism (Hartley 23-27).

Whom did you pick? Assumptions often lead us down the wrong path in observation. To avoid assumptions, ask clarifying questions, just as we learned earlier from Mr. Wallace. In a forthcoming chapter, *Technique – Listen Actively*, we will encounter more pointers on how to best take in what someone is saying. But by this point you should not be surprised that asking some good (and sometimes obvious) questions will be key.

My Episode Of ER

I can personally attest to this myself. For several years I have been participating with colleagues in an annual *Corporate Challenge* charity run for the YMCA. While the event draws some elite athletes who win effortlessly each year, the majority like me runs, jogs, walks, and pants its way through the five kilometre (roughly three mile) course down by Lake Ontario. In 2009, I felt that I had maintained a hard pace (for me anyways), and rewarded myself with a self-congratulatory attitude as younger colleagues struggled to keep up.

Well, they would have the last laugh. The next day I felt some chest pains that refused to subside so I reluctantly paid a visit to my local hospital emergency room. This was not my first visit to ER (I had a run-in with a ladder that nearly guillotined my thumb once) so I made sure to bring a fair amount of reading material for the anticipated multi-hour wait. Big surprise. I did not know that the best way to get to the front of the queue is to tell the triage nurse that you are experiencing chest pains. Within about five minutes of arrival I was whisked away for a battery of diagnostic tests. I actually heard one patient who had arrived ahead of me complain to the nurse as to why I would be served before him!

The whole sequence of events was such a blur. I had an intravenous line inserted in my right hand for potential IV drips, I was put in a glass-walled observation room with nurses and doctors coming in and out. There was a chest x-ray done, lots of blood work and possibly some other tests – it all happened fast, within a couple of hours.

The good news – I wasn't having a heart attack. Everything seemed normal except for one blood test that pointed to a kidney issue. I was referred to a specialist who would follow up in a few weeks. Curious, I consulted the real specialist – my mother – who assured me that there was no family history of kidney disease. So I trundled off to see my family physician.

With my test results in hand, he immediately asked me *one question*: "What were you doing the day before?" No one else asked me that question. Not one ER nurse. Not one doctor. Each highly trained professional had assumed that I had a cardiac issue and after that was eliminated, the assumption turned to a kidney problem.

But my local family doctor did not make this assumption. "What were you doing the day before?" I recounted that I was involved in the corporate run event. "Were you dehydrated?" was his next probing question. Hmmm … I thought back … I did not carry any water with me during the race and had a headache immediately afterwards. I supposed it was quite conceivable that I was dehydrated.

Just to be certain, my family doctor sent me off for a blood test – and it came back negative, meaning my kidneys were normal. The specialist never called back to confirm an appointment and just as well – the way things were going I might have ended up in surgery because most of the well-meaning acute care professionals were missing vital background data because they made an assumption instead of asking a clarifying question.

Rush To Judgment

My ER episode is nothing compared with the harrowing accounts of clinicians like Dr. Jerome Groopman.

"Not long ago I [Dr. Groopman] spoke with a middle-aged woman whose mother had been misdiagnosed with Alzheimer's disease. The elderly woman's memory was fading, and her family was close to admitting her to a nursing home. Luckily, the family decided to get a second opinion from a neurologist at a different hospital. It turned out the woman did not have Alzheimer's at all but, rather, vitamin B12 deficiency, a well-recognized cause of dementia. Her mild anemia, also due to vitamin B12 deficiency, had been written off by her internist as being due to 'old age.' Injections with the vitamin fully reversed the anemia and restored her thinking" ("Your Doctor and You – Why Doctors Make Mistakes ").

Dr. Groopman explains: "Unfortunately, medical misdiagnosis is not a rare phenomenon. About 15 percent of all patients are misdiagnosed, and half of those face serious harm, even death, because of the error. Contrary to the general impression that most misdiagnoses result from a technical foul-up, such as mislabeling someone's X-ray or mixing up a blood specimen in the laboratory, most cases are due to mistakes in the mind of the doctor" ("Your Doctor and You – Why Doctors Make Mistakes").

Dr. Groopman explains why misdiagnoses happen in his book, *How Doctors Think*. He runs through the dangers of incomplete observation or diagnosis, pinpointing what causes doctors to make assumptions or snap judgements:

- **Heuristics:** "Research shows that most doctors quickly come up with two or three possible diagnoses from the outset of meeting a patient ... All develop their hypotheses from a very incomplete body of information. To do this, doctors use shortcuts. These are called heuristics" (*How Doctors Think* 35). Heuristics are not bad, nor wildly inaccurate, but they are only an initial guess that demands deeper probing to substantiate the inherent assumptions.

- **Prototype:** This is basically a set of assumptions based on initial observations of a patient that appear consistent with representative cases. The problem is that prototypes can be wrong. Dr. Groopman gives the example of a seemingly healthy forest ranger who develops chest pains that are attributed (in the absence of traditional diagnostics like an ECG, chest x-ray, blood tests) incorrectly to over-exertion or muscle strain. The assumptions seemed justified because big, muscular, healthy-looking forest rangers experiencing distress must be suffering from physical over-exertion. The doctor used a prototype that caused him to fail to consider other causes of the chest pain, which turned out to be unstable angina. The assumptions allowed serious heart disease to be missed (*How Doctors Think* 44).

- **Explaining Away Abnormalities**: The story is told of a ten year old boy who collapses after some rough play during a "piggy back" ride. The initial diagnosis was that the incident was caused only by a single collapsed vertebra. While the boy's severe pain *solely* from an attempted piggy-back ride was unusual, it was dismissed by a doctor declaring "We just see this sometimes ..." (*How Doctors Think* 60).

In fact, the boy had a form of leukemia that affected his vertebra. A dismissive explanation demands continued observation in case the real problem is to be found elsewhere.

- **Anchoring**: This is "the tendency to grab on to the first symptom, physical finding, or laboratory abnormality. Such snap judgments may be correct, but they can also lead physicians astray" ("Your Doctor and You – Why Doctors Make Mistakes*").

- **Attribution**: "This accounts for many of the misdiagnoses in the elderly. Attribution refers to the tendency to mentally invoke a stereotype and 'attribute' symptoms to it. Alas, this stereotype is usually a negative one - an older person is labelled a complainer, a hypochondriac, or a person unable to cope with his or her naturally declining abilities. The doctor ignores the possibility of an illness that is not specifically *attributed* to 'old age' ..." ("Your Doctor and You – Why Doctors Make Mistakes*"*).

- **Availability**: This is another heuristic founded on "the tendency to judge the likelihood of an event by the ease with which relevant examples come to mind" (*How Doctors Think* 64). For example in a hospital emergency room, if there are a high number of flu cases presented, then a patient complaining of sore throat, fever, etc. will likely be diagnosed as having the flu.

- **Diagnosis Momentum**: Once a doctor arrives at a diagnosis, as he relays it to other doctors, those clinicians may simply assume the diagnosis is accurate without weighing any other evidence or confirming the original diagnosis for themselves. Thus, the assumptions of one doctor are assumed by each subsequent doctor (*How Doctors Think* 128).

- **Commission Bias:** Doctors may be biased towards taking action, any kind of action, before a complete diagnosis validates that the action is in fact the correct one. Dr. Groopman gives the example of a health issue he himself had with his hand. Surgeons examining him rushed to the surgical decision (*How Doctors Think* 169).

I have a nurse-friend who put it very plainly to me once: "If you go to see a surgeon, the surgeon will want to operate – that's what surgeons do!" Makes perfect sense. Visit a naturopath and see if surgery is ever recommended.

- **Distractions in the Emergency Room:** In the Emergency Room, doctors can be or seem rushed, "distracted, frequently interrupted by other doctors, nurses ... as he interviews or examines [a patient] ... a fair question to ask an emergency room physician is: **'What's the worst thing this [set of symptoms] can be? ... By asking that question [one] can slow down the doctor's pace and help him think more broadly"** (*How Doctors Think* 75).

"What we say to a physician, and how we say it, sculpts his thinking. That includes not only our answers but our questions" (*How Doctors Think* 76).

Before we go on, the diagnosis question suggested bears repeating. Later in this book, you will read about severe suffering endured by patients that might have been averted if the patients had asked that one simple question:

"What's the worst thing this [set of symptoms] can be?"

As I understand Dr. Groopman's intention, you do not necessarily even require an answer from your doctor to this question. Or the answer might be steeped in indecipherable medical lingo. *It does not matter. Just ask the question.* This forces a doctor to slow down and think rather than make hasty assumptions with your health.

I would suggest that you learn to ask yourself similar questions to slow yourself down as well anytime you are jumping to conclusions.

If you are serious about asking good questions to safeguard your personal health, you should look at the sample questions under Medical Diagnosis in the chapter *Jump Start With Attributes*. Dr. Groopman gives us some reassurance that all is not bleak in the medical world: "I have found that smart and dedicated physicians are able to explain their thinking, and they are able to put into clear and accessible lay language how they arrived at their working diagnosis. In some instances these questions [see the chapter *Jump Start With Attributes*] may cause the doctor to go back and re-examine assumptions, to think again, and to come up with a different, and now correct, diagnosis. All doctors want the best treatment for their patients, and the best treatment involves the most open-minded thinking" ("Your Doctor and You – Why Doctors Make Mistakes").

Second Opinion

Thankfully, there are also other strategies to counter our tendency to make assumptions. Dr. Groopman advocates thinking out loud when you observe something unknown. He recounts an incident with a newborn patient whose blood vessels were not routed as they should be, resulting in inadequate oxygen being supplied to the baby. The other clinicians were focused on the failure of the pulmonary veins which normally would carry oxygenated blood from the lungs into the left atrium of the heart. However, the doctor who solved the mystery injected dye into the infant's pulmonary artery whereupon he was quite surprised to see that the dye ended up in the baby's stomach where it should *not* have been.

"What doesn't belong here?" [the doctor] asked himself (*How Doctors Think* 144). Since he was facing an unknown, he thought out loud. Once he realized that the there was a problem with the baby's blood vessel routing, the baby was saved through surgery to correct this.

Furthermore, the doctor commented: "'When a case first arrives I don't want to hear anyone else's diagnosis. I look at the primary data' ... when one piece does not fit, he seizes on it as the key to unlock the mystery" (*How Doctors Think* 146).

Dr. Groopman concludes by stating that "Creativity and imagination, rather than adherence to the obvious are needed in situations where the data and clinical findings do not all fit neatly together" (*How Doctors Think* 171).

Bucking The Trend

To reiterate, in this chapter we can glean at least four principles from Mr. Wallace and Dr. Groopman to counter assumptions:

1. Slow down.
2. Think out loud.
3. Ask clarifying questions.
4. Be creative.

Over the years, while I have made (and continue to make) too many wrong assumptions, I have at least learned to automatically question some common place assumptions. Take the example of a company looking for a business partner. Most people immediately assume that the best partner is the biggest company in its sector. That means if you are looking to market a new fast food menu idea, you would call up McDonalds before Burger King. However, in my experience, the *second place* company generally makes a better partner.

I think it was in the 1970s that car rental company, Avis, ran a successful advertising campaign proclaiming "We're number two, we try harder". This was a gutsy plan because it flouted the traditional wisdom that if you were in second place, you should not draw attention to it. But the plan was effective, overcoming the brand value of number one Hertz, even with (their now infamous) pitchman O.J. Simpson hurdling and hurtling through airports.

This same perception - that any company that isn't number one would be more aggressive, more focused, more hungry, and more risk-taking in order to get to number one - stuck with me and is one of my selection criteria whenever I am looking for business partners.

Not Assuming and the Queen

When I learned that the High Commission of Canada decides who receives an invitation to the Queen's Garden Parties, I knew I could not assume that every applicant would be invited.

Once I made a connection with the High Commission I began my onslaught of questions, one specific to how many Canadians typically make the cut. When the answer came back that only about two hundred Canadians make the list each year, I realized how small my odds were to succeed. To make matters worse, the High Commission also informed me that their selection process would be by random lottery if too many applications were submitted.

Well that revelation did not sit too well with me. But in the spirit of this chapter's topic, I would not allow myself to assume that these rules were unchangeable. Regardless of how Garden Party invitees might be selected, I decided that I had better start differentiating myself from the other applicants in the hope that this might help my cause. This determination prompted me to send a copy of the response letter from Lady Susan Hussey directly to the High Commission to make it known that I had received some modest recognition in the Palace organization.

And concerning that package I had dispatched to the Queen - its contents were also shaped by the questioning of assumptions. When I did my initial royal research, I learned that Her Majesty is not an avid reader. Her father, HRH King George VI once famously instructed his daughter's tutor to simply focus on making sure that her handwriting was legible. However, I later discovered that the Queen *does* like reading – well, at least she likes to read Dick Francis mysteries, and hence my inclusion of one of Mr. Francis' novels.

Chapter 13

TECHNIQUE – WATCH YOUR LANGUAGE

Action At Last

We now move to the third segment of the APT approach to better observation – technique. This is last in order because people tend to rush to be able to *do* something without first knowing the background principles behind the techniques.

FIGURE 13-1 The APT Principles

A **ATTITUDE**	Be Curious Be Creative Be Persistent Be Thorough Be Skeptical
P **PREPARATION**	Have A Specific Objective Do Your Homework Know Your Audience Choose The Right Person Don't Assume
T **TECHNIQUE**	Watch Your Language Listen Actively Soften Up Your Audience Ask Short Simple Questions Look for Inconsistencies

Once I was attempting to help one of my kids with math homework. Well, being a "mathie" I have been trained to always do things from "first principles", meaning you are always going back to basics first and then deriving the result based on these principles. This apparently does not go over well with teens. Especially with teens who are not mathematical – and who have a big assignment due the next day.

Nonetheless here was my opportunity. "Would I help with a math problem?" I was asked. With pleasure. But not thirty seconds into my mini-trigonometry lecture, I was fired. That has never happened before. I was replaced by a co-dependent high school classmate on the phone who had equal challenges with math. "Why?" I asked. "I just want to get the *answer*" was the reply.

You may be cut from the same cloth – you want to know "*how*" rather than "*why*" - so I need to congratulate you for sticking with me this far. That is, unless you skimmed through the previous chapters to arrive here ... in which case I urge you to go back and cover the earlier material first – it takes longer, but if you really want to observe better then – well – you should not skip half of the observations on the subject!

Lingua Franca

Growing up as a so-called Chinese-Canadian I had to explain hundreds of times to native Chinese speakers that I could understand seventy percent of what they say, but could not speak Chinese very well (if your family immigrated from another country, you know what I mean). The first time I visited Hong Kong I had repeated embarrassment in retail store after retail store as the salespeople seemed to sneer at me – "you look Chinese, so why can you not speak Chinese?" – that is what I thought they said anyways from the seventy percent I could comprehend! As much as I resented being treated as a "second class citizen" I could not deny the fact that language is a bridge when you use it properly and a barrier when you do not.

Therefore, this chapter is about language, but the language I am talking about is actually not Chinese, English, Spanish, or Swahili. Every culture, every community, every vocation has its own "secret" vocabulary – the jargon or lingo that separates insiders from outsiders. It is this special language that you need to be aware of, you must learn, and you must use if you want to reach the objective of your questions.

You may remember that after my initial stint as a college math instructor, I landed in the software business. The software industry is steeped in its own peculiar language. You might think that you are already pretty tech-savvy – after all, if you've ever had to remove a virus from your home computer or install a wireless router, or even setup a home theatre, you know that technology is everywhere and demands expertise from everyone. But there's lingo and then there's lingo.

In my first interview for a software developer position, I was asked to explain twenty-five technology acronyms. We're not talking about the easy ones like "CPU" (central processing unit) or "RAM" (random access memory). No, I was asked about insider vocabulary like the following:

- X25
- SNMP
- RUK
- LIFO
- APR
- MMU

Recognize any of these? I confess I made one of the terms up – but do you even know which one?

That interview was another bump in the road of my education in observation – learn the language and use the right language. I think out of twenty-five acronyms I got twenty-four wrong. If you want to go deeper with technical people, you have to "talk the talk".

With technical language things become even more difficult because there are essentially different *dialects*. I remember being educated in the trenches working with IBM as a business partner (I picked them because they were *number two* in the area we were working in, using the principle in the previous chapter). After a number of months recording my own notes on terminology that I was picking up, I was fairly proficient using the right lingo to build deeper relationships with IBMers (that term is part of the lingo too). If you were walking into a meeting with an IBM field sales team in 2005 you would immediately ask for the CE's SSSR and ITS to agree on whether to pitch the current release of DB2, with or without the latest Fix Pack, or push the upcoming GA. Comprendo?

Just as this all became second nature, we signed Microsoft as another partner, forcing me to learn a whole new dialect. Just like learning a second language, I was constantly translating terms between IBM and Microsoft usage.

In case you are interested, here's a translation of some of the IBM terms and their Microsoft equivalents:

TABLE 13-1 IBM and Microsoft Terminology

IBM Term	Microsoft Term	Meaning
CE – client executive	AM – account manager	The sales professional who owns the overall sales quota for a specific customer.
ITS – information technology specialist	TSP – technical sales professional	The technical sales professional who works with multiple customers to convince them of the technical merits of a specific set of products.
Fix Pack	Service Pack	An interim software release that adds incremental improvements and/or repairs identified problems.
GA – general availability	RTM – release to manufacturing	Major software release, ready for production environments.

Now it's not just with geeks that your choice of language will either open or close doors for your questions. Suppose for example you are talking (or should I say texting) to a bunch of teens. See if you can decode the following texting acronyms:

- LOL
- TTYL
- ISH
- JIC
- NRN
- TTTT

I remember once giving a workshop to a group of teens. Struggling to establish some common ground, I attempted to make a point using the acronym *PDA*. Instead of heads nodding I saw startled faces. Finally I asked what the problem was and one teen explained that PDA means "personal display of affection". Hmmm ... the last time I used that acronym it meant "personal digital assistant" (today you'd call this a "smart phone"). Watch your language!

Stop right now and think about your world and the special terms that you use every day. Can you come up with a list of six or more words or phrases with little effort? Suppose you are preparing to interview a famous chef like Gordon Ramsey. Alright, I know that he *really* should watch his language since his "special vocabulary" is mostly expletives — but where would you turn to quickly find a list of basic culinary words or concepts so that the interview with Chef Ramsey would sound coherent? I would probably begin by reading food reviews or watching some cooking shows. In a later chapter, *Jump Start With Attributes*, I suggest that by knowing six basic facts about a particular subject you can get a foothold in a discussion on that topic. You'll be able to validate this hypothesis by visiting my upcoming website, www.6basix.com to contribute your own "six basic attributes" on any subject that interests you, from skydiving to sushi.

By the way (and note I did not use the shorthand "BTW") ... in case you are wondering, here is the decoding of the six texting acronyms I threw at you earlier:

- LOL (laugh out loud)
- TTYL (talk to you later)
- ISH (I'm so hungry)
- JIC (just in case)
- NRN (not right now)
- TTTT (too tired to talk)

Language Sensitivity

With language, even as you strive to learn it and use it properly, there is always room for misinterpretation. This is why in the next chapter, *Technique – Listen* Actively, it is also essential to confirm that what you *think* you are hearing is really what the speaker intends to convey.

Harvard's Dr. Jerome Groopman underscores the importance of language in medical practice: "While modern medicine is aided by a dazzling array of technologies, like high-resolution MRI scans and pinpoint DNA analysis, *language* [italics added] is still the bedrock of clinical practice. We tell the doctor what is bothering us, what we feel is different, and then respond to his questions" (*How Doctors Think* 8).

And again from Dr. Groopman: "Here is the art of medicine, the *sensitivity to language* [italics added] and emotion that makes for a superior clinician" (*How Doctors Think* 22).

I read an advertisement titled *Choose Your Cruise* that makes for a simple exercise for you to see how sensitive (or not) you are to language (i.e. can you "read between the lines"). See if you can infer what the ads are *really* telling you:

TABLE 13-2 Analyzing Language: Comparing Advertised Cruises

	Royal Caribbean International	**Oceania Cruises**
The Offer	"Known for innovative ships offering rock-climbing walls, ice-skating rinks, inline skating tracks, bungee trampolines, and the Flowrider surf simulator, Royal Caribbean is one of the biggest names in cruising. This line, with its mammoth ships, appeals to families, couples and singles who want to do, see and experience all the top Mediterranean ports of call, plus an amazing onboard experience" ("Choose Your Cruise").	"For seasoned cruisers looking for a destination-intensive experience, Oceania Cruises is a popular choice. With its small fleet of luxurious 684-passenger ships, this cruise line focuses on getting to those Mediterranean ports that larger ships just cannot reach. Clients love the top-notch food and highly personalized service, all at a mid-market price" ("Choose Your Cruise").
What Are They *Really* Saying	I interpret that the ship is better than the ports of call, that in fact, the ship is the real destination. Look at all the references to the ship's amenities in contrast to a single lonely mention of the Mediterranean:	I interpret that the ports of call are the focus, and that the ship isn't the big attraction. Right at the top they say they offer a *"destination-intensive experience"*. Sounds positive, but look at all the back-handed

Technique – Watch Your Language

	Royal Caribbean International	Oceania Cruises
	"innovative ships"; *"rock-climbing walls, ice-skating rinks, inline skating tracks, bungee trampolines, and the Flowrider surf simulator"*; *"mammoth ships"*; *"amazing onboard experience"*; Perhaps you'd have just as much fun in this ship if it never even left the harbour!	swipes they take at competitors like Royal Caribbean in an attempt to set themselves apart as exclusive: *"For seasoned cruisers"* (i.e. novices are attracted to the bells and whistles of other more ostentatious ships); *"... small fleet"* (i.e. they don't have a lot of ships, but somehow theirs are better); *"... 684-passenger ships"* (i.e. they don't cram them in like the 3000 or more that would travel with Royal Caribbean); *"... getting to those Mediterranean ports that larger ships just cannot reach"* (i.e. they can go further inland on smaller waterways); There is no mention of onboard amenities maybe because they couldn't put that many on their smaller ships.

	Royal Caribbean International	Oceania Cruises
		Perhaps it would be better to fly because you can get to the destinations faster!

Body Language

If "actions speak louder than words" then body language is like the "ninth part" of speech. We all know that we can pick up a lot more meaning from a conversation when we are face-to-face with our audience, reading what is being conveyed without words through body position, gestures, and facial expressions.

This is why, despite the technological advances, the big marketing push, and the incentive of saving on travel budgets around video conferencing, the good old fashioned meeting is still the best way to conduct business.

The first and so far only visit I ever made to Malaysia was precisely for the extra value of human proximity. Our software startup was making inroads in international sales. Asia, however, is an extremely difficult place to do business. Discount expectations are outrageous (about seventy percent to start), time zone differences are harsh (twelve plus hours ahead of east coast time), language is non-alphabetic, and culture can be a complete mystery. And getting there is half the fun.

Fortunately, IBM was footing the bill for this Malaysian junket so at least I could enjoy the seventeen hour flight from Toronto to Kuala Lumpur (KL) in business class. I departed on a Sunday morning

Toronto-time, arrived early evening Monday KL-time, had my two hour meeting on the Tuesday afternoon, and was back on the plane Wednesday morning. So the cost was really four days of my time, ten thousand dollars of our business partner's cash – all for a two hour meeting with an Asian bank executive.

Internet presence may be shaking up electronic commerce, but *people* still do the buying and the selling, and there is no substitute for doing business in person.

Interpreting body language is not only the domain of business. In medicine, Dr. Groopman explains that "The physical examination begins with the first visual impression in the waiting room ..." (*How Doctors Think* 12).

Nurses are trained similarly to observe patients' body language. In *Physical Examination & Health Assessment,* Carolyn Jarvis advocates factoring in non-verbal body language in patient assessments. Basically, there are five types of nonverbal behaviours that convey information about the person (Jarvis 58-59):

- Vocal cues, such as pitch, tone, and quality of voice, including moaning, crying, and groaning.
- Action cues, such as posture, facial expression, and gestures.
- Object cues, such as clothes, jewellery, and hairstyles.
- Use of personal and territorial space in interpersonal transactions and care of belongings.
- Touch, which involves the use of personal space and action.

In preparing cross-examiners, George Colman writes in *Cross-Examination – A Practical Handbook* about the importance of scrutinizing body language to identify any inconsistency or inaccurate testimony:

> Counsel's concentration on the subject-matter of the evidence should be combined with *close attention to the manner* [italics added] in which it is presented. He should watch the witness ... interested in what is emphasized, but equally interested in what is unemphasized, omitted, or slurred ... There may be, somewhere, an usually long pause, a hesitation, the drawing of a deep breath. The witness may be seen to swallow hard; he may change his tone, or he may take a hurried glance at someone other than the person who is questioning him. Counsel may notice some nervous gesture with a hand or a shoulder which appears at certain stages. (Colman 62)

Media interviewers like Larry King paid close attention to body language. Mr. King was once asked about what he learned from his friendship with actor Marlon Brando (star of the 1972 film *The Godfather*): "Marlon and I were having dinner and he pointed out a couple nearby. 'They're not happy,' he said. 'How do you know?' I asked. 'Look at the way the guy crosses his leg, and how he looks over her shoulder, not at her face.' His [Mr. Brando's] genius came from observing people" (King 246).

I trust the point is clear - use the language of your audience, and read their body language and you'll gain credibility, earn goodwill, and infer insights that will permit you to get further in your questioning and hence towards your objective.

Watching Your Language And The Queen

Since all of my communications to this point with Buckingham Palace, the Governor General, and the High Commission have all been by phone, letter, or email, I have not been able to take advantage of body language.

In my letter to the Queen (see the earlier chapter *Attitude – Be Thorough*), I did spend a good amount of time trying to craft my *diction*, to use language that would convey meaning with Her Majesty. For example, I made a point to incorporate the word "duty" – it is clear from following the Queen that if nothing else, she has been exemplary for her decades of sacrifice and service for the sake of duty to her nation, to the Commonwealth, and to the throne.

The tone I employed in all communications was as deferential as I could make it. I presumed nothing and only requested consideration to be invited to meet with the Queen in as gentle a manner as possible (the image of monarchs ordering subjects beheaded for insolence to the throne was front and centre!).

I also had to take considerable care to get all the titles correct – so there were a number of "HRHs" (His Royal Highness or Her Royal Highness) and other inclusions of formal titles. This whole protocol thing can be quite exhausting!

But the last thing I wanted was to have my letter rejected. As you now know, I had success in guiding my letter into the right hands. Whether that would be enough in my queenly quest remains to be seen.

Chapter 14

TECHNIQUE – LISTEN ACTIVELY

Left And Right Again

Listening is a skill that many women insist men need to improve on. I speak from experience and confess that at times I do try to multi-task when listening to someone else speak (how about you – are you listening to music, eating, talking on the phone as you read this book?). Rudeness is not intended but that seems to matter little as the person doing the speaking can usually tell when the person doing the listening isn't.

In defence of the male part of the species, I found an interesting theory as to why men in general may tend to be "listening-challenged". In the book *Listen Up,* social scientists Dr. Larry Barker and Dr. Kittie Watson explain that "men listen with half a brain" (Barker, and Watson 128). Stop right there - yes, I realize this explanation is like throwing gasoline on the fire, but we should hear the authors out.

Dr. Barker and Dr. Watson cite brain research suggesting that "When most men listen they process language using the left hemisphere while women process language through both the right and left hemispheres. In fact, baby girls have a larger connector between the right and left hemispheres that allows data to move easily between hemispheres ... [on balance, the authors add that] It appears that men are better able than women to tune-out distractions. Since women naturally use both hemispheres to process information, they are more easily distracted by competing messages than men" (Barker, and Watson 128-132).

Whether you accept any of these theories or not, we need to treat them as intended – as explanations, not excuses. Male or female, we can improve our listening skills, and in so doing, we will also improve our observation skills.

Take The Test

Here's a little self-evaluation test on your attitudes and behaviour towards listening from *The Business Of Listening* (answer Yes or No to each question):

1. I am interested in many subjects and do not knowingly tune out dry-sounding information.

2. I listen carefully for a speaker's main ideas and supporting points.

3. I take notes during meetings to record key points.

4. I am not easily distracted.

5. I keep my emotions under control.

6. I do not fake attention.

7. I wait for the speaker to finish before finally evaluating the message.

8. I respond appropriately with a smile, a nod, or a word of acknowledgment as a speaker is talking.

9. I am aware of mannerisms that may distract a speaker and keep mine under control.

10. I understand my biases and control them when I am listening.

11. I refrain from constantly interrupting.

12. I value eye contact and maintain it most of the time.

13. I often restate or paraphrase what the speaker said to make sure I have the correct meaning.

14. I listen for the speaker's emotional meaning as well as subject matter content.

15. I ask questions for clarification.

16. I do not finish other people's sentences unless asked to do so.

17. When listening on the telephone, I keep one hand free to take notes.

18. I attempt to set aside my ego and focus on the speaker rather than on myself.

19. I am careful to judge the message rather than the speaker.

20. I am a patient listener most of the time.

According to author Diane Bone, here's what your scores mean (44):

- 1-5 "No" answers: You are an excellent listener.

- 6-10 "No" answers: You are a good listener but can improve.

- 11-15 "No" answers: Through practice you can become a much more effective listener.

- 16-20 "No" answers: You need to work on listening.

Is Anybody Listening Out There?

My first trip through my public library's online catalogue hinted at a broader (gender neutral) listening problem. First, most of the books on the topic of listening were sitting on library shelves waiting to be read – so very few people were taking these books out. Second, many of the books were written for those who are new to the English language (i.e. English-as-a-second language aka ESL students). Great that *ESL* students are learning to listen, but not so great that as soon as a person graduates with a command of the language, listening falls out of favour.

It is almost as if listening is second class – if you are in a conversation and are unfamiliar with the language or the topic of discussion then you are resigned to be the listener. But once you know a thing or two, then you go on the offensive and speak more than listen. Richard Harris puts it this way in his book, *The Listening Leader*. "Speech is power ..." (4).

If you have ever sat through any kind of government proceedings, you know about the decline of listening. One of my sons served as a Legislative Page one year in our provincial body of government (the Ontario Legislature) so I was invited to sit in the public gallery on one occasion - there would be no second occasion! Aside from the thrill of seeing my son and his young colleagues scurrying around the parliamentary benches, the legislative debates were numbingly banal. Members of the Legislature would rise and drone on with wordy attempts to embarrass their opposite number. No one really listened as responses to these barbs typically ignored the original question altogether. I do not know how *C-Span*, a US-based public affairs TV broadcaster, can have any viewing audience. I can just imagine the confusion for an ESL student who might unwittingly tune in.

Open Invitations

Gordon MacKinnon's book, *Investigative Interviewing*, tells us that "... the art of listening [is the] key to the role of the investigative interviewer". He goes on to cite the "80/20 rule", i.e. that an interviewer should talk no more than twenty percent of the time (13-14).

In his work training medical students, Dr. Groopman commented that "very bright and very affable medical students, interns, and residents all too often failed to *question cogently or listen carefully or observe keenly* [italics added] ..." (*How Doctors Think* 4). Doctors are often taught to work through checklists in diagnosing patients. But Dr. Groopman observes that "Lists are useful, and like algorithms can make care more efficient in certain circumstances, yet they also pose the same risks, that the doctor will not ask ... open-ended questions ..." (*How Doctors Think* 88).

Here's an example of an open-ended question vs. a closed-ended question:

Closed: "Have you finished studying for your math exam?"
Response: "Yes."

Closed-ended questions invite "yes/no" answers that are devoid of insight and context. A better rephrasing would be:

Open: "How are you studying for your math exam?"
Response: "I am working through my old assignments."

The open-ended question has left the door open for additional questions (like "Which assignment is giving you the most challenges?") that build on the details offered up in the previous responses. Open-ended questions allow for the responder to tell you things that might not be volunteered otherwise.

As we will see, open-ended questions invite exploration that demands good listening skills to piece together conclusions from all the responses.

Listening Can Save Lives (Really)

In a real-life story that I have retold to many people, Dr. Groopman had given the account of a woman who had suffered from a debilitating illness for fifteen years. This woman was the patient of many specialists, and the diagnoses were as varied as the doctors themselves: she had severe eating disorders, and/or a failing immune system, and/or irritable bowel syndrome. Any one diagnosis would be terrifying enough. As this woman desperately searched for an accurate diagnosis, she dropped to a weight of eighty-two pounds (about thirty-seven kilograms).

As we learned in the earlier chapter, *Preparation – Don't Assume*, well-trained and well-intentioned doctors can sometimes arrive at incomplete or incorrect diagnoses owing to factors like heuristics, prototype, explaining away abnormalities, availability, diagnosis momentum, commission bias, and distractions in the ER room.

This terrible decline in the woman's well-being occurred over a fifteen year period until one day she finally met a gastroenterologist who did something the other doctors failed to do: "... [this doctor] began to *question, and listen, and observe* [italics added], and then to think differently about [her] case. And by doing so, he saved her life, because for fifteen years a key aspect of her illness had been missed" (*How Doctors Think* 1-3).

Apparently, one of the many doctors in her past had wrongly concluded that this woman suffered from an eating disorder – the root cause was singled out as psychological, not physiological. Dr. Groopman shares that this patient was increasingly shunned, even mocked, when she continued to return to the emergency room after another severe episode. She was labelled as a troublesome patient who simply needed to change her diet and eat at least three thousand calories per day (that's about twice the normal calorie intake recommended for a middle-aged woman of moderate height, weight, and activity level), with an emphasis on pasta to get her body weight back up ("Canada's Food Guide").

Try as this woman did to follow this dietary advice, she just became more and more ill. Her very life was increasingly in danger. Finally, this one solitary observant gastroenterologist came to the correct diagnosis – he discovered that the woman had celiac disease, a severe allergic reaction to gluten (*How Doctors Think* 1-3).

Gluten. One of the principal ingredients in pasta - which one of her prior doctors advised that she needed to eat lots of, to the tune of twice the normal calorie intake for healthy women. And she nearly died as a result because her root problem was an allergy to this very ingredient.

This story horrifies me. The explanation that Dr. Groopman offers as to how all those well-trained medical professionals had failed this woman is as follows: "... how a doctor asks questions and how he responds to his patient's emotions are both key to what [researchers] term 'patient activation and engagement.' ... Observers have noted that, on average, physicians **interrupt patients within eighteen seconds** *of when they begin telling their story* [bold face and italics added]" (*How Doctors Think* 17).

As I had already pointed out in *Preparation – Don't Assume*, I want to repeat Dr. Groopman's advice again because it is that important:

When you are being diagnosed by a doctor, ask the simple question:

"What's the worst thing this [set of symptoms] can be?"

The intention of this question isn't necessarily to receive an answer. You are only trying to help your doctor to *slow down and think* – to take more than eighteen seconds with your health.

However your doctor responds to this question, you will transform the diagnostic process into a diagnostic *conversation*. It is your body, your health, and you know how you feel better than anyone else. It is the doctor's job to listen to you, but it is your job to help the doctor to listen.

Active Listening

In *The Listening Leader*, business communications specialist Richard Harris offers up a number of practical means for us to improve our listening. Here is a sampling of Mr. Harris' suggestions:

1. **Interact With The Speaker:** A listener should interact with a speaker's message "through restatement, acknowledgement, and questioning" (Harris 15). In other words, when you listen, you are not passive. You can draw out more from the speaker by verbalizing back what you think you are hearing and asking follow-on questions that serve to both acknowledge that you are really listening, and seeking to clarify. In these ways, you confirm that what you *think* you are hearing is what the speaker is trying to convey.

2. **Don't Rush To Judgment:** It is a common temptation to draw premature conclusions with partial information. The listener's mind works faster than the speaker's mouth. However, if you interject with a premature judgment, you may cut off communications and hence curtail anything you might actually learn otherwise (Harris 15).

3. **Make Eye Contact:** This is a tough one for Asians who were raised to believe that looking someone in the eye is disrespectful. Nonetheless, Mr. Harris points out that almost ninety percent of information conveyed in face-to-face conversation comes first through what we see. By looking the speaker in the eye, you also increase your chances of focusing on what the speaker is saying (Harris 38).

4. **Take Notes:** Where possible, if you are taking notes (not doodling or writing out a grocery list) you will more likely absorb what the speaker is saying (Harris 60).

5. **Reflect Feelings:** If the speaker expresses emotions, the alert and attentive listener will echo these back empathetically. This creates an emotional connection that signals that you are not only listening for information, but perceiving the speaker's feelings about that information.

For example, if someone tells you that he had a terrible time driving in rush hour traffic to make a meeting with you, a dismissive response would be "Let's get started." A better response would reflect empathy: "That must have been a big pain – I hate rush hour traffic too. Thanks for going through all that to meet with me" (Harris 68).

So Listen Up

In *How To Interview – The Art of the Media Interview,* Paul McLaughlin emphasizes that "If I could write only one chapter about interviewing it would be about listening. And if I could write only one sentence, it would be this. The more deeply you listen, the more eloquently people will speak" (1).

Part of good listening is to become comfortable with silence, not feeling compelled to fill the sometimes uncomfortable void with chatter. This in fact is something I have learned in teaching – too many new teachers lead students in the responses they want to hear whenever there is a lull. Yet silence is not the teacher's enemy, but the teacher's ally – silence deepens reflection.

Mr. McLaughlin states that: "A speaker who's been delivering a contrived response has nothing prepared to fall back on when greeted with silence [from you, the listener] ... [So] If the speaker takes the plunge and continues to talk, what comes out is likely much closer to the truth" (6).

Listening And The Queen

Sometimes the biggest impediment to listening is not wanting to hear what is being said. If we put a positive spin on this, it's called stubborn optimism. If we call it as it is, we might say it is denial. In either case, the result is the same – avoidance of the facts.

In the 2006 Hollywood film, *The Queen*, the storyline portrays Her Majesty as having misread the depth of emotion and attachment that the British public had for Princess Diana. In the film, the British Prime Minister Tony Blair repeatedly pleads with Buckingham Palace to acknowledge the public outpouring of grief and to permit a public ceremony marking the Princess' funeral.

By the way, in a twist of "life imitating art", the screenwriter of *The Queen* had allegedly accused the real Mr. Blair of taking lines straight out of the film script and claiming that he originally spoke them verbatim. Now why Mr. Blair would ever want or need to do this is a bit perplexing.

But the script does an admirable job of illustrating the importance of listening. In the film, only when the royal family accepts the public's demands and *listens* to them does a modicum of respect return to the monarchy.

Back to real life now. My self-imposed challenge to try to find some way to meet with the Queen. may seem presumptuous – maybe even preposterous. However, with typical naïve zeal, I believed I would be able to engineer a meeting. This was certainly my expectation when I sent the package to the Queen. In fact, in my letter (see the end of the chapter *Preparation – Be Thorough*) to Her Majesty, I directly asked for an opportunity to present a book (actually *this book*) to her in person. Blame it on all the years I spent in sales.

You can imagine I found it difficult to accept that I had to trust my chances of meeting the Queen, directly or otherwise, to a third party, the High Commission of Canada in London. But as I look back, I was referred to the High Commission not once, not twice, but three times by:

1. The Governor General of Canada
2. "Jane Smith"
3. Lady Susan Hussey

The detailed chronology of these responses was already presented in the chapter, *Preparation – Choose the Right Person*. I did not want to trust my chances to someone else, but in the end I had no choice but to listen. Once I accepted this, however, I then stepped up my correspondence and follow up with the High Commission. As an anecdotal measure of success in that department, I went through the many emails sent back-and-forth between me and the High Commission and I noticed a pattern in the salutations.

The initial communications with the High Commission started with:

- "Dear Mr. Albert Lee" (sounds like a stiff computer-generated automated response)
- "Dear Mr. Lee" came next (formal, but more human), and then
- "Dear Albert"

I wouldn't dare to expect that the next salutation might be "Dear Al" or "Hey Al", but by listening to the multi-sourced advice and accepting the selection protocol I am at least winning some favour, however fleeting.

Chapter 15

TECHNIQUE – SOFTEN UP YOUR AUDIENCE

Choose Your Softener

This chapter is almost entirely driven by what I learned from media interviewers – David Frost, Larry King, Mike Wallace, and Barbara Walters. "Softening up your Audience" might sound a tad offensive, but just as a professional interviewer has to open up his guests in order to go deeper, so we too need to put our audience at ease lest our questions deflect off the protective shell that enshrouds most people.

The actual approach you use will depend on your personality. As we have seen, Mr. King likes to use warmth and congeniality to prepare the way with his guests whereas Mr. Wallace preferred to soften his guests up about as subtly as the way an air force "softens" up its enemy by bombing. Either way, the purpose is the same – to get beyond the superficial.

For me, I tend to turn to humour, especially the self-deprecatory type. I have found that making fun of me sets people at ease so that they will lower their guard. On top of that, there are other benefits in not taking yourself too seriously. I tell my children all the time that they must be able to laugh at themselves – this grace empowers us to be more resilient when we face failure.

For example, take the way I walk (please!). If you took a book and balanced it on the head of most people, it would stay pretty much at the same height from the floor as the person traversed a room. Me? You could become motion sick watching the book undulate up and down. I just have trouble walking properly. I attribute my bobbing gait to my father but perhaps it is as much the result of being patently un-co-ordinated.

So people laugh at me all the time. People imitate me (with pronounced exaggeration for added effect). I am pretty certain that the little smile on the face of total strangers who pass me on the sidewalk is not because of some stand-up routine on their iPod. Call me hyper-sensitive. Call me clumsy. It doesn't matter – I accept my shortcomings and I leverage them to disarm people.

Get The First Laugh

Piers Morgan, the British personality (former editor of *News of the World* and *The Daily Mirror*, and celebrity judge on *Britain's Got Talent*) and successor to Larry King on CNN, shared a similar approach to softening up his guests.

When Mr. Morgan was asked about the secret of good interviewing he replied: "You've got to start with a good laugh. You've got to make your interviewees feel at ease, and laughter is the best way of relaxing anybody. And I like to suddenly out of nowhere *ask a tricky question* [italics added], with no point to it at all, because that's how you *get the right answer* [italics added]."

As an example of a tricky Piers Morgan question, consider this exchange with Mr. Morgan as the interviewee:

[Interviewer] What was the best question you asked Oprah?

[Mr. Morgan] The best thing I asked Oprah, which totally took her by surprise, was, 'How many times have you properly been in love, where your heart aches and breaks?' It was a great question for Oprah, because she's never been asked it. Her answer was fantastic.

[Interviewer] What was her answer?

[Mr. Morgan] I won't tell you. (Ryan 4)

Surprise Attack

More "sophisticated" people than me employ other means of softening, some more underhanded than others. When I was in high school, video games were just emerging on the scene. Atari had released Pong, its iconic black and white paddle tennis game. Our school was looking for ways to generate extra income for programs (not much has changed since then) and so our students' council had the idea of installing a coin-operated Pong game. I actually wrote up a proposal to our district school board to lobby for approval.

One evening, our school had a community "open house" event. An older woman made her way to me and started talking about the video game standoff. She empathized with me regarding our uphill battle with "those big bad politicians" and in so doing, she led me to open up and give her my unvarnished view of things. Turns out she was our school board trustee – i.e. one of the "big bad politicians". I had no idea. I felt sheepish and deceived, but she certainly knew how to soften up her "opponent" to draw out what I was really thinking.

In cross-examination, lawyers take a different but equally revealing tack. Cross-examiners are trained to ask unexpected questions to uncover the truth. George Colman reveals in his book *Cross-Examination – A Practical Handbook*, that "... usually it is possible, in cross-examination, to ask [the witness] questions which he has not expected. In order to deal with these, he [the witness] may have to improvise. And in so doing, he is not unlikely to say something which counsel will be able to reveal as untruthful or improbable ..." (28).

David Frost used similar cross-examination style tactics to pin down former president Richard Nixon in Mr. Frost's famous interviews. The unexpected questions came by way of Watergate trial prosecution exhibits uncovered by Mr. Frost's researcher, Jim Reston. These exhibits caught Mr. Nixon off guard. That element of surprise enabled Mr. Frost to draw out some astounding acknowledgements of wrongdoing by Mr. Nixon (Frost 18).

I suggest you read Mr. Frost's book, *Frost/Nixon – Behind The Scenes Of The Nixon Interviews* for a complete play-by-play account. The condensed version of how Mr. Frost softened up the wily and combative Mr. Nixon goes like this:

- Mr. Nixon had, from the time of the actual Watergate trial (1973) to the time of the Frost/Nixon interviews (1977), denied that he had ever obstructed justice during the cover-up of the Watergate break-in that was orchestrated by senior White House staff.

- However, Mr. Frost used his research material to confront Mr. Nixon. Reference was made to taped conversations between Mr. Nixon and his special aide, Charles Colson, that indicated Mr. Nixon knew about the break-in as early as three days after it had occurred. This taped evidence surprised Mr. Nixon since he was unaware that Mr. Frost possessed it. Even though Mr.

Nixon tried to recover with steadfast denials of any intent to cover-up, he was on his way down (Frost 104, 211-213).

- Mr. Frost moved on to question Mr. Nixon over the payment of "hush money" to keep one of the Watergate break-in defendants quiet. Mr. Nixon again tried to avoid responsibility for these payouts by saying that "I [Mr. Nixon] didn't endorse or ratify it [the "hush money"]" (Frost 111). But Mr. Frost softened Mr. Nixon up further by responding with: "'Why didn't you stop it?' Again the question jolted Nixon" (Frost 232).

- In the next interview session, "Nixon, finally, began to crumble." Mr. Nixon resignedly started to accept responsibility, saying: "Let the bad come out ... there's plenty of bad. I'm not proud of this period. Ah ... I didn't handle it well. I messed up" (Frost 115).

- Mr. Frost had Mr. Nixon on the ropes and continued to press, insisting that Mr. Nixon needed to go further than only admitting that "mistakes" were made (Frost 242).

- Mr. Nixon lamented: "I brought myself down. I gave them [the impeachment lobby] a sword. And they stuck it in. And they twisted it with relish" (Frost 122).

- And then out came Mr. Nixon's deepest confessions of questionable conduct and cover up: "As the one with the chief responsibility for seeing that the laws of the United States are enforced, ***I did not meet that responsibility*** [bold face and italics added]. And, to the extent that I did not meet that responsibility, to the extent that within the law, and in some cases going right to the ***edge of the law*** [bold face and italics added], in trying to advise Ehrlichman and Haldeman [two of the accused White House staffers in the Watergate trial] and all the rest as to how best to present their cases, because I thought they were legally innocent, that I came to the edge. And under the circumstances, I would have to say that a reasonable person could call that **_a cover-up_** [italics and bold face added] ... I let down my friends. I let down the country. I let down our system of government and the dreams of all those young people that ought to get into government but think it's all too corrupt and the rest. ... Yep, I ... I, I let the American people down. And I have to carry that burden with me for the rest of my life. My political life is over" (Frost 123-124).

These admissions were dramatic admissions that had previously never surfaced, despite the political and legal zeal of US congressmen, senators, prosecutors, and reporters. But Mr. Frost, a one-time TV game show host, was able to extract these revelations from a shrewd and adept former president because Mr. Frost knew how to soften up his audience.

We are seeing a pattern here – the use of surprise is a favoured tactic by many in preparing an audience to open up. Larry King joins the bandwagon with a twist in that he himself also wants in on the surprise: "The key [to spontaneous interviewing] is the element of surprise .... me, I'm seventy-five years old and I still want to be surprised every night. When I'm surprised that's when I know I'm doing my show right" (King 134).

Provocateurs Extraordinaire

Barbara Walters, long-time anchor of ABC's *20/20* news program disclosed that: "A humanized and deliberately *provocative question* [italics added] has fewer snares [than asking celebrities routine and mundane questions about their best-known work]. Ask a painter what is the most beautiful thing he has ever seen. Ask a writer how he first broke into print. Ask a musician if it is a waste of time to go to the symphony if the music seems meaningless. Ask him how to inspire children to appreciate music. Ask him if music is an acquired taste" (Walters 15).

Mike Wallace of *60 Minutes* is by now familiar to us as a sometimes abrasive, "in your face" style of reporter. He employed surprise also, but the surprise usually had an edge to it as well. On one occasion after Mr. Wallace asked some very pointed questions of Ronald Reagan during Mr. Reagan's first US presidential election campaign, Mrs. Nancy Reagan confronted Mr. Wallace. Mr. Wallace responded "that in asking the kind of questions that upset her, I was merely doing my job" (58).

Here are some other examples of how Mr. Wallace softened up his subjects with his investigative reporting style:

- "In an effort to get under [Anwar] Sadat's skin a bit [Mr. Sadat was the President of Egypt], I [Mr. Wallace] asked him if he was aware that he was often referred to in those days [when Mr. Sadat was chief deputy to Gamal Abdel Nasser, Egypt's ruler] as 'Nasser's poodle, Nassser's Mr. Yes-Yes.' [Sadat agreed after a moment with a smile]" (Wallace 111).

- "[Mr. Wallace, speaking to the newly installed Ayatollah Khomeini of Iran] Imam, President Sadat of Egypt, a devoutly religious man, a Muslim, says that what you are doing now is – quote – 'a disgrace to Islam.' And he calls you, Imam – forgive me, his words, not mine – 'a lunatic' " (Wallace 129).

- Mr. Wallace had asked the mother of recording diva Barbara Streisand if she was close to her daughter. Ms. Streisand's mother responded: "She hasn't got time to be close to anyone". Then Mr. Wallace repeated this back in an interview with Ms. Streisand herself. "Streisand began to cry, and as she wiped the tears from her eyes, she said, 'You like this, that forty million people have to see me, like, do this' " (Wallace 240).

Well, after learning about some of the "tricks of the trade" to soften up audiences, I can understand why the Queen resolutely refuses to give media interviews! Yet the take-away here is that you can waste a lot of time making polite conversation and make no progress towards your objective unless you also learn how to open up your audience. You do not need to be abrasive – remember you can use humour and take a softer approach to softening. But soften you must.

Softening Up Your Audience and the Queen

You have already seen the letter I sent to the Queen (see the chapter *Attitude – Be Thorough*). While you might have expected me to use humour to open up a dialog with the Queen, the homework I had done warned me to keep to proper protocol and deference, so humour was out.

Instead, I employed another popular way of softening up an audience – creating a bridge via common acquaintances. Even a total stranger will think twice about deleting your unsolicited email or hanging up on you if you mention a name that the stranger recognizes from his personal network.

Given that we know that the Queen receives so much correspondence that she has a typical three week backlog to contend with despite having office staff and Ladies-in-Waiting to assist her, I figured I had better do more than simply mention names. So for each person from my own network who had some connection with the Queen, I also tried to deepen the connection through references to her father and son.

Technique – Soften Up Your Audience   191

These are the people I cited:

- A friend who was a student nurse in London in the 1950s who trained at the Brompton Hospital where she encountered Her Majesty's <u>father, King George VI</u> as a patient being treated there.

- An acquaintance who had been a classmate of her <u>son, Prince Andrew</u> at Lakefield College in Peterborough, Canada.

- My very own niece, who had been selected to present flowers to <u>Her Majesty</u> during a stop on her 2002 visit to Toronto, Canada.

Did my attempts prove fruitful? Only a royal "fly on the wall" in the Palace knows for sure. At least I know that *someone* spent a good amount of time looking at my package to the Queen, as we will find in the coming chapters.

Chapter 16

TECHNIQUE – ASK SHORT SIMPLE QUESTIONS

Easy As Duct Tape

Duct tape is one of those simple, fix-all, bring-with-you-everywhere kind of items. Duct tape was used to jury-rig a carbon dioxide filter on the crippled Apollo 13 spacecraft, one of many engineering quick fixes devised ingeniously to bring the astronauts home safely ("The Frustrations of Fra Mauro: Part I").

And duct tape reminds us that simple solutions can be elegant solutions.

Or more to the point, simple questions can also be effective questions. That doesn't mean that simple questions should be *simple-minded*. I already discussed open-ended questions as preferable to closed-ended questions, since the latter usually only draw out a yes/no response. In the chapter, *Preparation – Have a Specific Objective*, we saw how *60 Minutes'* Mike Wallace asked hard hitting questions to elicit a response. Mr. Wallace's questions were not long and complex, they were short and to the point, in fact to a very sharp point.

Less Yields More

Larry King has the experience to do this well. In his book, *My Remarkable Journey*, he confides:

- "All I do is ask questions, *short, simple questions* [italics added]. Once I had a specialist on the show about diabetes. I asked him what the word 'diabetes' meant. He said 'I learned it my third day of medical school and no one has asked me since.'"

- "Why do we want to hunt animals?"

- "Why do you take pictures?"

- "What happened in the war today?"

Simple questions often get surprising answers [italics added], but you really have to listen when you interview like that [i.e. asking simple questions without any presumption, spontaneously without preparation] because your next question always depends on the last answer" (King 133-134).

When technology superstar Steve Jobs returned to Apple in 1997 after his first parting, he did not recognize the company that he had founded. In part due to a high number of mediocre products, the one-time upstart computer manufacturer was plummeting towards bankruptcy. In his biography of Steve Jobs, Walter Isaacson quotes Mr. Jobs: "I had people explaining [all the different versions of the new Macintosh computer] to me for three weeks. I couldn't figure it out." Mr. Jobs decided to *simplify* his questions by asking "Which ones do I tell my friends to buy?" (Isaacson 337).

Keep It Simple (Not Stupid)

Paul McLaughlin continues this theme in *How To Interview – The Art of the Media Interview*. "Don't be afraid to ask 'simple questions.'. People often equate simple with stupid, which is a mistake. One of the hardest standards to achieve is simplicity. Anyone can hide facts by hiding behind verbose language and complicated questions. Clarity and conciseness, on the other hand, is harder to achieve and requires considerable effort" (139).

To ask simple questions doesn't mean that you'll get back simple answers. Mr. King shares that "One of the things I always try to do is ask questions that begin with the word **why** [bold face and italics added]. A why question can't be answered in one word" (King 243).

In the medical field, open-ended questions can be simple and straight-to-the-point. *Physical Examination & Health Assessment* by Carolyn Jarvis states: "The open-ended question asks for narrative information. It states the topic to be discussed but only in general terms. Use it to begin the interview, to introduce a new section of questions, and whenever the person introduces a new topic. The open-ended question leaves the person free to answer in any way … It lets the person express herself or himself fully" (Jarvis 54).

Here are some examples of simple questions in a medical patient interview (Jarvis 54):

- "Tell me how I can help you."

- "What brings you to the clinic (or) hospital?"

- "Tell me why you have come here today?"

- "How have you been getting along?"

- "How have you been feeling since your last appointment?"

- "What has been most challenging?"

- "What would you like to be able to do, change, or address?"

- "What stands out for you as really important for me to know about your situation?"

Do Not Try This At Home

In contrast, there are bad ways of asking questions. Not only are closed-ended questions poor (remember, the ones that elicit a yes/no response), but asking a leading or biased question also takes you nowhere. Ms. Jarvis gives the example of a poor question to ask a male patient in a medical interview: "You don't smoke, do you?"

So how do you think the patient will respond? The phrasing of the question implies that one answer is better than another. Even if the answer is given honestly, the patient will likely become guarded, pre-empting the flow of important information required for an accurate diagnosis (Jarvis 57).

Shortened Story

Striving for the simple and elegant continues to be a learning experience for me too. Sometimes when I ask a question, I receive a quizzical look that tells me to rephrase. The challenge of simplicity is not so much about what to say, but what *not* to say.

I remember the first time I learned the importance of the "customer value proposition" (CVP). I was running business development for the software company where that big quarter of a million dollar deal came in unexpectedly from Chase Manhattan Bank. In those wild early days of figuring out how to sell products we needed a lot of hand holding. Well, in retrospect, we were in pretty good hands.

Back in about the year 2002, we had hired on Robert Herjavec to help bring a sales focus to our fledgling software business. If you've ever watched ABC's *Shark Tank* or CBC's *Dragons' Den*, you will recognize Mr. Herjavec as one of the celebrity judges of the pitches unleashed by sometimes zany entrepreneurs on each TV show. I remember the very first session held at seven in the morning. Mr. Herjavec asked each member of the executive team to verbalize what was so compelling about our products, i.e. what did each of us think the CVP was? I remember that my answer was very forgettable!

The idea behind a CVP is to be able to express in one short sentence why a customer should care about your product or service. Everyone likes to point to one-time legacy film giant Kodak, whose famous CVP was "We capture your memories forever." In an earlier chapter I referred to car rental agency Avis and their CVP "We're number two, we try harder."

The key to CVPs is to keep them short and to put in only the bare essence – anything else will not stick in the customer's mind. Sales people employ a similar device called an "elevator pitch" – a short, punchy paragraph that conveys their message in the time it takes to get on and off an elevator.

We had a challenge to convey our software product CVP in only a few words – technical people like to tell you at length about all the nuances of their software, often to their peril.

Deciding what to put in and what to leave out requires us to know our audience and to do our homework, so if you need a refresher, stop here and go back to those earlier chapters.

I know I may already have dredged up unpleasant memories for you when I had made earlier references to math and doing homework, but since things always seem to happen in threes, I have one more school experience to inflict on you – the précis.

Are you back now from tearing out your hair (or the pages of this book)? The term "précis" is an older one and students today might know this by other names like a summary or a condensed version of some literary work. When I was in school, we were taught to take a short piece of writing, say six paragraphs long, and shorten it down to one paragraph. The trick is to try to retain all the essential points while cutting out the rest. To succeed, you had to become adept at the art of summarizing - compressing multiple words into as compact an expression as possible. I believe that if you learn to do a proper précis, you will be able to ask good simple questions that get to the heart of a subject.

For example, take the paragraph above that you just finished reading. A reasonable précis of this paragraph would be:

Learning to write a précis, a condensed summary of the most important points, is helpful in coming up with simple questions.

The original paragraph consists of 136 words. The précis uses only 21 words – a compression of about one-sixth. You might find this easy, or you might find this difficult. If you are in the latter camp, you should realize that you are probably creating précis all the time, and you are also likely better at it than you think.

For example, think of the last film you watched (in the theatre, or more likely on your computer or TV). Tell me what the movie is about. Unless you took two hours and a bucket of popcorn to respond, you just gave me a précis of the movie. Did you leave out a bunch of details? Of course you did (and I hope you left out how the film ends so you do not ruin it for me!).

In the earlier chapter, *Preparation – Be Curious*, we formulated some questions to give some structure to curiosity using the tried and true questioning paradigm of *Who, What, Where, When, Why, How*. When doing a précis, you will find that if you concentrate on summarizing *Who* (who is the main character in the piece you are summarizing) and *What* (what is the main plot or main message) you will do just fine.

So to ask simple questions, do your preparation work on the subject, pick your specific objective, and then zoom in on the shortest, simplest, most essential questions you will need to ask to achieve your objective.

Perhaps the best example I can give you is to recount for you how this all played out in the context of my quest to meet with the Queen.

Asking Short Simple Questions And The Queen

First, let's review what we know from my *preparation* work:

- Correspondence with the Queen is managed by "Jane Smith", who decides what letters will be read by the Queen.

- The Queen is private and only meets with those whom she invites. Strict protocols are in place.

- The Queen's annual Garden Parties are the only predictable venue for a "commoner" to meet the Queen.

- There are typically only four Garden Parties a year.

- Canadians are only given on average about fifty invitations per Garden Party, and these invitations are awarded solely at the discretion of the High Commission.

Second, let's remind ourselves what the *objective* is: to try to meet with the Queen.

Third, who is the *Right Person* to ask my short, simple questions to? In the earlier chapter, *Preparation– Choose the Right Person*, I formed the list of six people that I had to navigate through:

1. Buckingham Palace Operator
2. Governor General's Office of the Secretary
3. Canadian Heritage inquiries staff
4. High Commission, Royal Events Co-ordinator
5. "Jane Smith", Palace Information Office
6. Lady Susan Hussey, Woman of the Bedchamber

Now I had to consider my specific objective, *to try to meet the Queen*, and decide what I needed from each person in my list of six to get me closer – in effect, I had to figure out a smaller objective for each person. To simply blurt out "What's the best way to meet the Queen" with the Buckingham Palace Operator would not go over too well I am sure!

Here is what I came up with:

TABLE 16-1 Short Simple Questions to Reach the Queen

Audience	Objective	Simple Question	Response
Buckingham Palace Operator	To speak to someone closer to the Queen for any help on how to meet with the Queen	May I speak to someone in the Palace Information Office? [initially I did not know if "Jane Smith" would work, so I asked a general question].	The Operator wouldn't let me through – she asked what the inquiry was concerning so I mentioned I was sending the Queen a book and asked for confirmation of the mailing address.
Governor General's Office of the Secretary	To get a direct invitation to a Garden Party	Does the Governor General make recommendations of Canadians to attend one of the Queen's Garden Parties?	I was referred to Canadian Heritage.
Canadian Heritage inquiries staff	To find out if there's any alternative to	Are there any visits from the Queen scheduled	The Queen had no scheduled

Audience	Objective	Simple Question	Response
	Garden Parties to meet the Queen	for 2011? Who would I speak to regarding the process of being invited to one of the Queen's Garden Parties?	visits to Canada in 2011. I was referred back to the Governor General regarding my Garden Parties question.
Governor General's Office of the Secretary	To clarify the process to get invited to a Garden Party	I was sent from your office to Canadian Heritage and back to you again! Could you provide guidance on how to be invited to the Queen's Garden Party?	I was referred to the High Commission.
High Commission, Royal Events Co-ordinator	To get special consideration for an invitation to a Garden Party	What is the process to be considered for invitation to one of Her Majesty's Garden Parties?	I finally learned of the whole protocol for invitations. As I got further with "Jane Smith" and after

Audience	Objective	Simple Question	Response
			receiving a personal response from Lady Susan Hussey, I updated the High Commission about all this progress so that they would see that I'm not your everyday average royal watcher. The High Commission actually commented that I did indeed receive a very "nice" letter from the Palace.
Buckingham Palace Operator	To get to "Jane Smith"	May I please speak with "Jane Smith" of the Palace Information	This time the Palace Operator put me

Audience	Objective	Simple Question	Response
		Office?	through.
"Jane Smith", Palace Information Office	To raise my profile in the Information Office in order to somehow increase my odds of selection.	I am calling to confirm receipt of a book I sent Her Majesty three weeks ago. How long does it take for a response, and would it be by mail as we have a mail strike in Canada? [Response] Mail dealt with in order of date rec'd; What is the right way to be considered for the Queen's Garden Parties?	I was told of a backlog in mail responses due to the recent royal wedding. The backlog is more than three weeks now; normally it takes two-three weeks for a response. She suggested I contact the Governor General's office.

From the responses to my *simple* questions, you have a sense of what progress I was able to make – slow but steady, and very much a step-by-step process, with each successive question adding a bit more insight to the previous responses.

Chapter 17

TECHNIQUE – LOOK FOR INCONSISTENCIES

Something Doesn't Add Up

We have now reached the final technique in the APT Principles, and as was the case for the other two segments (Attitude, Preparation), the last principle is always a "negative" one. So here we are not creating new ideas and methods to fuel our questions, but checking that the responses our questions elicited make sense.

Just as accountants always aim to balance the books and math students are exhorted to double check their answers, so we are looking for consistency – and when something does not add up, does not fit, is not consistent – that is a clue that we may actually learn something significant.

In the online article, *Samuel Weiss: Science And Serendipity*, contributor Shawn Lawrence sums this concept up: "It is a proven fact that in the scientific world of controlled experiments, behind a surprising number of scientific breakthroughs, there are a number of lucky accidents. In fact, scientists have come to some of their most important findings while they're off looking for something else entirely. While it is important to appreciate that serendipity does play a role in science, progress is also the result of rigorous research, analysis and the ability to uncover the answers in the *small things that don't add up* [italics added]" (Lawrence).

Mr. Lawrence goes on to highlight the discovery by Dr. Samuel Weiss, a Canadian neurobiologist, and his colleagues, that adult stem cells exist in the brain. Dr. Weiss is quoted saying "We were actually investigating how to use growth factors to protect the brain. That's when we found cells in the brain that seemed to behave like stem cells. We did some experiments and confirmed it - they were indeed neural stem cells" (Lawrence).

Talking about clues, if you like mysteries, then you may have seen the 2009 Hollywood film *Sherlock Holmes*. In the title role, actor Robert Downey Jr. masterfully solves a string of murders by a twisted aristocrat, Lord Blackwood, bent on seizing political power by deception. Early on, Lord Blackwood is executed (or so we think) yet he somehow dramatically reappears to continue his murdering spree. Throughout this time, Lord Blackwood convinces everyone that he possesses mysterious dark powers that have enabled him to return from the dead to kill all who oppose his ambitions – everyone that is except Sherlock Holmes. Mr. Holmes follows the evidence trail to a laboratory with a number of puzzling experiments in progress. The inconsistency of Lord Blackwood's apparent execution and resurrection leads Mr. Holmes to deduce that these lab experiments are the real power behind each fraudulent "supernatural" act.

Interviewer Larry King is also particularly good at exposing details that do not fit together, citing on one occasion: "… Brooklyn had taught me how to ask good questions like 'How could that new restaurant be called the 'Famous' when it just opened?'" (King 53).

In his line of questioning, a cross examiner is constantly looking for inconsistencies. George Colman shares some of his favourite cross-examining questions to flush out faulty evidence: "Among the many types of detail which can be used to test the reliability of evidence [i.e. to expose inconsistency], dates and the sequence of events may be important ... witnesses cannot always remember dates accurately, and may be careless of them when fabricating ..." (Colman 30).

Just as we had learned in the chapter *Attitude – Be* Skeptical – if you weigh what someone is telling you like a cross-examiner, you will constantly be trying to validate the facts, looking for inconsistency.

Three Sides

Flushing out inconsistency can be very helpful in other applications too such as marital counselling. As one of my pastors used to say "There are always three sides to every story – his side, her side, and the truth."

When quarrelling couples rehash some unresolved dispute, you can always count on the fact that only one side of the story will come out – his or her side of the story - so inconsistencies will abound. Just the other day my two kids were out playing ice hockey at the local rink. The youngest one returned home first, without his older brother. Apparently there was an altercation (again), and the account was told of how the older one was at fault – he allegedly refused to give the younger one his hockey puck back and then to boot, the older one supposedly speared the younger one with a hockey stick.

I've heard enough of these sad tales to know I should reserve judgment until the other side is told. Sure enough, when the older one returned, his story was a tad different. Yes, there was a fight over a hockey puck, but that arose because the younger one stopped cooperating and picked up his puck (the only puck) to leave, leaving the older one "out of puck" (sorry, couldn't help myself).

The truth is somewhere in between as any parent will tell you. When the stories do not add up, there is truth to be found if you are on the lookout for inconsistencies.

Spotting The Spot

Do you remember that horrific account from Dr. Jerome Groopman that was told in the chapter *Technique – Listen Actively*? A woman had been deteriorating rapidly after fifteen years of suffering apparent eating disorders only to finally be diagnosed correctly as having celiac disease.

Dr. Groopman writes: "Everyone had written her off as some neurotic case. But my intuition told me that *the picture didn't entirely fit* [italics added]. And once I felt that way, I began to wonder: what was missing?" (*How Doctors Think* 20).

It was the final recognition of an astute specialist that saved this patient – he weighed the medical evidence and had to conclude that something did not fit.

On a similar theme but on a much more tragic scale, there was a recent report in *Christianity Today* documenting the terrible suffering of about one million Ethiopians from a disease called Podo, which can cause the feet to deform into a rotting, smelly, cauliflower-like state.

"It seems to afflict those that walk on red volcanic mountain soil, but many doctors had misdiagnosed the symptoms as 'infectious elephantiasis' until a Christian doctor named Ewart Price realized that the *diagnosis didn't fit* [italics added]. Using geological maps, Dr. Price connected the symptoms to Ethiopia's volcanic soil. Then, examining tissue samples, he found tiny silica crystals embedded in the victims' lymphatic tissue. He guessed that the silica found its way through the skin of the feet and ended up scarring or blocking lymphatic channels, causing swelling and deformity" (Stafford).

Looking For Inconsistencies And The Queen

Do you remember the letter I received back from Buckingham Palace (see the chapter *Preparation – Choose The Right Person*)? Lady Susan Hussey refers to the Queen fondly recalling her visit to Canada in **2002**. Seems like a polite and proper little tidbit to offer up. I did not think anything of this for several months until I was actually writing this chapter.

Finally it dawned on me that something did not add up.

In my original letter (to which Lady Hussey was responding), I had mentioned that my niece had presented flowers to the Queen – the proof was in the accompanying photo that I had sent with the letter. But I never specified the date of that royal visit – in fact, I myself did not even know the date. I checked a copy of the photo that I had sent with the letter – it had no date stamped on it.

I pulled out a copy of the letter I had sent with the photo. That's when I realized I was *wrong* in my letter – in it I had written that my niece had presented flowers "on [the Queen's] most recent trip to Canada". Fine enough, except that the Queen's most recent trip was in **2010**. And before that she had been to Canada in **2006**. But my niece did the honours in **2002**.

So how exactly did Lady Hussey deduce that my niece had met the Queen in 2002? Not from my letter and not from the photo. Did she know based on the gown that the Queen was wearing? Or the crown she was donning? Or from the Queen's appearance? Does the Palace keep an archive of photos of every presentation to the Queen that someone (maybe "Jane Smith"?) had to search through for a match?

I have no idea how Lady Hussey figured the photo was (correctly) from 2002. It is a mystery. But I see this *inconsistency* as further evidence that my letter and package were carefully scrutinized by the Queen and her staff. And one of my details (the photo) included to soften the way was noticed. Everything counts.

Chapter 18

JUMP START WITH ATTRIBUTES

Twenty Questions

As we have now seen, the APT Principles can help equip you to ask good questions to deepen your observation in any subject area, from medicine to scams, from job interviews to media interviews. However, suppose you are facing a subject that you know absolutely nothing about? To dive into the fifteen APT Principles without at least some background knowledge of the subject would be folly.

For example, I do not know a whole lot about cars. When I buy a car, I always bring it back to the original dealer who sold it to me. I used to do my own car repairs when I had a "lemon" that I bought back in university – but in those days cars *could* be maintained by amateurs. Now everything under the hood is computerized and specialized so there's not a lot of tuning that can be done with a wrench and "elbow grease".

Not long ago I had an intermittent car problem – sometimes the engine would just stop running – I would hit the gas pedal but instead of speeding up, the car would slow down and then grind to a halt, and always in traffic of course. Somehow I coaxed my car to make it all the way back to my dealer. The technician at the counter asked me to describe the problem. I tried, but did not get too far because my car vocabulary was stuck in the 1980s ... when I suggested a carburetor problem it was game over ... no one told me that modern cars do not have carburetors anymore!

My failure stemmed from not knowing the basics of how a modern car engine works. To communicate effectively with my mechanic, I did not need to be an "Indy 500" pit specialist, but I did need to know five or six things about engines. Unfortunately, I was four or five facts short.

What I needed was a jump start (pun intended). When facing a new subject for the first time, you cannot use the APT Principles very well without first acquiring some basic knowledge of the subject. Without these basics, the questions you do ask will be vague and will probably miss the mark.

When I work with children to teach observational skills I often will use a simple game I call "Twenty Questions". I'll bring in some mystery object (which means the students know nothing about the "subject") and then unveil it with a flourish – the students then have a few minutes to come up with at least twenty questions about the object to try to guess what it is.

Suppose the object is a water bottle:

FIGURE 18-1 Water Bottle

Source: Copyright Anthony Hall/Shutterstock.com. Used by Permission.

Time yourself for two minutes and see how many questions you can come up with. Here's what I came up with:

TABLE 18-1 Water Bottle Attributes

Number	Question	Attribute
1	What kind of metal is it made of?	Construction
2	Is the cap screwed on or pulled off?	Usage
3	How tall is it?	Dimensions
4	What is the capacity?	Dimensions
5	Can you put hot and cold	Usage

Number	Question	Attribute
	liquids in?	
6	Will this set off a metal detector?	Construction
7	How much does it cost?	Cost
8	Where can I buy it?	Supplier
9	Who makes it?	Supplier
10	How strong is the seal?	Construction
11	Is there an aftertaste?	Usage
12	Does it have any HBAs?	Construction
13	Where is it made?	Supplier
14	Does it come in other colours?	Construction
15	Is it easy to dent?	Construction
16	Can it go in the dishwasher?	Usage
17	Will it fit in my backpack's mesh side pocket?	Dimensions
18	What liquids can go in safely?	Usage
19	Who else has one?	Owners
20	Does it come in see-through plastic?	Construction

Now, you might think this is just another exercise to hone your question-asking ability. Well, it never hurts to practise, but in this case, the questions are *not* the main focus.

Six Attributes

You'll notice that I added a third column to this table, *Attribute* – this is a fancy word for a quality or descriptor of an object. These attributes will jump start the questioning process.

Think about eggs: they can basically be described by these attributes:

- origin (chicken, quail, ...)
- habitat (free range, ...)
- size (small, large, ...)
- grade (A, AA, ...)
- colour (white, brown, ...)
- additives (omega-3)

Everything can be described by its basic attributes. Are you meeting a stranger for lunch? You can describe her by her height, build, age, hair style, and so on. Looking for a condo? You'll want to know its location, number of bedrooms, what floor it is on, listing price, age, amenities, and so on. If every object is a noun, then all its possible adjectives are its attributes.

So returning to the water bottle exercise, I took the twenty questions I came up with and *classified* them according to what attribute they relate to.

As it turns out, the unique attributes for a water bottle that came out of my twenty questions are:

- Construction
- Usage
- Dimensions
- Cost
- Supplier
- Owners

To simplify your attribute hunt, I have a totally unscientific hypothesis: most subjects can be loosely described with **about six attributes**. Using the water bottle example again, I'm saying that you will have a good initial idea of all the essential details of this object by knowing about the six attributes: construction, usage, dimensions, cost, supplier, owners.

For example, suppose I told you that the water bottle matches this description:

TABLE 18-2 Specific Attributes of a Water Bottle

Attribute	Value
Construction	Made of stainless steel
Usage	Used only for holding cold water
Dimensions	About 15 cm. (6 in.) tall, with a volume of about 600 mL (20 oz. US)
Cost	About ten dollars
Supplier	Made by New Wave Enviro
Owners	Carried by health-conscious commuters

You now know most everything you need to know about the water bottle. Of course there are other attributes, but these are the basics. And by the way – the first twenty questions I devised for the water bottle are the ones I noted for you above and when I grouped these into attributes, I actually came up with exactly six attributes.

Since I began this chapter talking about cars, allow me to leave you with one more example of the automotive kind. I recently tried to sell my (not-always-so-trusty) car. When I posted my ad to craigslist I was asked to describe the car, i.e. to list its attributes:

- Make
- Model
- Year
- Mileage
- Colour
- Price

I could have included other attributes like options (four wheel drive, air conditioning, power locks etc.) but without the six attributes I listed, no one would have a clue as to what I was selling. With these six attributes, car hunters could decide if they wanted to ask for additional attributes or pass on the car altogether.

Quick, Search For Some Sushi

Another exercise you can do is to perform a search using your favourite internet search engine like Google or Bing. If you are searching for, say, a good Japanese restaurant, what happens if you simply enter "Japanese restaurant"?

When I did this in google (and by the way use the url https://www.google.com so that it is not localized to your home country like google.ca for Canada) I got back 19,500,000 hits. At that rate, you will never find a restaurant near you!

So what do you do normally? You narrow down the search criteria. How? By entering more key words – i.e. more *attributes*. When I started supplying more attributes, I got much closer to tasting some wasabi:

TABLE 18-3 Finding a Japanese Restaurant

Search Key Words	Attributes	Hits
"Japanese restaurant"	Cuisine	19,500,000
"Japanese restaurant" Toronto	Cuisine, city	948,000
"Japanese restaurant" Toronto "Yonge & Sheppard"	Cuisine, city, neighbourhood	58,100
"Japanese restaurant" Toronto "Yonge & Sheppard" LCBO	Cuisine, city, neighbourhood, liquor licensed ("LCBO" is the Liquor Control Board of Ontario)	2,320
"Japanese restaurant" Toronto "Yonge & Sheppard" LCBO Ichiban	Cuisine, city, neighbourhood, liquor licensed, name	5

Eye Spy

If you need more convincing that attributes are so fundamentally descriptive and prescriptive, you should read *Blink* by Malcolm Gladwell, a staff writer for *The New Yorker*. *Blink* is about "rapid cognition" – the ability to make the right decisions and assessments based on initial impressions made over very short time-frames. This is what Mr. Gladwell calls "thin slicing".

Evidence of rapid cognition is given via an account of an experiment by psychologist Samuel Gosling. Eighty college students were selected and then assessed by close friends using a "Big Five Inventory" questionnaire that focused on five areas: extraversion, agreeableness, conscientiousness, emotional stability, and openness to new experiences.

Next, Mr. Gosling took total strangers who had never met the students. By contrast with the group of close friends, these strangers were asked to spend only fifteen minutes to look at a student's college dorm room. Afterwards, the strangers also assessed the students in the same five areas.

Whose assessments were most accurate?

In three of the five inventory areas, the *strangers* were more accurate than the close friends. Mr. Gosling explained that "a person's bedroom gives three kinds of clues (think of these as three *attributes*) to his or her personality":

1. Identity Claims, i.e. how we would like others to see us (e.g. if you observe a framed Harvard degree on the wall, this suggests what the owner wants you to conclude about him).

2. Behavioral Residue, i.e. tell-tale clues of how one really behaves (e.g. dirty laundry strewn on the floor vs. a CD collection stored in alphabetical order are candid lifestyle clues to what a person is really like).

3. Thoughts & Feelings Regulators, i.e. what we do to our rooms to impact how we feel (e.g. a scented candle or stylistically placed pillows on a bed).

According to Mr. Gosling, knowing these three attributes lead to a surprisingly accurate personality profile (Gladwell 34-37).

Attributes and APT

Now you could quite rightly interject here and say that identifying the basic attributes is simply part of doing your homework as described in the Preparation segment. However, I wanted to single out the importance of knowing basic attributes because this is more than a preparation principle, it is a simple way of rapidly sizing up any subject to enable all of the APT Principles to go to work.

Of course like anything "simple", an over-emphasis on attributes can become *simplistic*. Clearly, fields of study that experts spend a lifetime in cannot be reduced to six attributes. But I still contend that a "quick and dirty" high level synopsis of a field of study can be reasonably represented by no more than six basic attributes.

Who Chooses The Six Basics

But who decides which six basic attributes are the best? Good question. If you are looking for a Japanese restaurant, you might value location over price. A student might rank price over number of menu items. The fact that experts often disagree with one another is not news. Every subject garners diverse opinions on what is most important.

I suggest that the best way to refine which attributes are most apt is to turn to the online community. Watch for a new website, www.6basix.com, that will let you contribute and retain your own basic attributes for any subject you are interested in. Visitors to the site will be able to add their own subjects and attributes and peruse the ones present. The web community will decide whose expertise is most useful – and it will be useful. Think of it like a condensed version of Wikipedia so that you can drop down into any of the many subjects and come out seconds later with just the key attributes you need so you can get a handle on any subject without getting handed too much detail.

Below is a collection of some of the basic attributes I have come across for a wide diversity of subjects (I really mean wide – from cheese tasting to safe sleepovers). The attributes may be given as statements or as questions. As already pointed out, there may not always be exactly six attributes – but usually six is about the right number – enough detail to be of use but not so much that it becomes unwieldy.

TABLE 18-4 Basic Attributes For Sample Subjects

Subject & References	Basic Attributes
Arson Investigation (Pepper 92-95)	- Background: Fire combustion "requires heat, fuel, oxygen and a source of ignition". - Source: Where a fire originates is called the "seat of fire"; e.g. where a scene shows the most "deep seated burning" indicates where the fire has burned longest, which may lead to discovery of things like matches or other intentional tinder material in the vicinity and hence a theory of arson. - Motive: If normally present valuables are missing (e.g. a television set in a living room) then it could point to an arsonist who first removed valuables prior to setting a fire. - Evidence: If a fire shows telltale signs of great severity or rapid progressions and spread, this could indicate that some type of accelerant was used, which would be another indication of arson. - Evidence: If a liquid fuel accelerant (like gasoline or paraffin) was used, there "will typically [be] a pool burn on the surface on which it has been burning. As the vapour from the liquid fuel burns it creates a pool or halo shape on the surface."

Subject & References	Basic Attributes

Cheese Tasting
 	
(Riedl)
	Suggested attributes and questions to evaluate cheese:
	
	- Appearance
	  - What colour is the rind?
	  - Is it moist, dry or cracked?
	  - Smooth or ridged?
	  - Thin or thick?
	  - What does it make you think of – tree bark, velvet, earth?
	  - What colour is the paste?
	
	- Aroma
	  - Close your eyes and wait for your first impression
	  - Aroma will help determine taste
	  - Smell cheese with the rind and without
	  - Note the intensity
	
	- Texture
	  - Is the paste firm or runny?
	  - Are there eyes in it (small holes like in Emmenthal)?
	  - Does it crumble when it breaks, or is it supple?
	  - Is it rich, silky?
	  - Does it coat the mouth?
	
	- Taste
	  - Does the cheese have a bitter finish?
	  - Is there a sweetness to the paste?

Subject & References	Basic Attributes
	- Is it tangy or salty? - Sharp or mellow? - Are the flavours balanced – salt, sweet, sour, bitter?
Child Abuse Prevention ("3 Steps For Choosing A Child Safe Organization")	To determine if the organization you work for is committed to child protection, ask these questions: - Training: Does the organization train staff about child sexual abuse? - Expectations: Does the organization have a code of conduct outlining boundary expectations between adults and children? - Screening: Does the organization have screening and hiring processes for staff/volunteers? - Reporting: Is there a process in place for staff/volunteers to report misconduct? - Policies: What is the organization's policy for reporting child abuse?

Subject & References	Basic Attributes
Crime Scene Investigation (burglary) (Pepper 13)	These are questions that should be asked by investigators at the scene of a burglary: - Entry: "Where and how did the intruder get into the premises?" - Exit: "Where and how did the intruder get out?" - Past: "Where has the intruder been?" - Items: "What has the intruder taken?" - When: "When did it happen?" - Discovery: "When did they find the burglary or theft?" - Witnesses: "Did anyone see the intruder? If so, have they spoken to the police?" - Scene: "When were the windows and doors last cleaned? This question will assist in providing a time frame during which the evidence such as blood or fingerprints could have been deposited."

Subject & References	Basic Attributes
Cross-Examination (Colman 66)	Here are some W5+H questions that cross-examiners should consider asking witnesses: - "How did he come to be there?" - "What was he doing?" - "How much would he have seen, heard, noticed?" - "Why does she remember that?" - "What would she have done if that really happened?" - "Whom would she have told?" - "How did they find him?" - "Why should he lie?" - "How does she know that?" - "How will it affect him if I lose this case? – How if I win it?" - "What makes you remember that so clearly?"

Subject & References	Basic Attributes

Dating
 	
("29 Dimensions of Capability")
	Online dating sites vary in the attributes they focus on to find matches for their clients. I was appalled that dating site Match.com only asked about four attributes in their "background/value" questions: ethnicity, religion, language, education.
	
	According to site eHarmony, there are twenty-nine attributes that lead to a good match. These attributes are supposed to help identify the following important factors:
	
	- Core Traits
	  - Emotional temperament
	  - Social Style
	  - Cognitive Mode
	  - Physicality
	
	- Vital Attributes
	  - Relationship skills
	  - Values and beliefs
	  - Key experiences

Evaluating REITS ("Real Estate Investment Trust")	REITs are "real estate investment trusts". According to the reference, the basic attributes to check out are: - NAV: Net asset value - FFO: Funds from operations - AFFO: Adjusted funds from operations - CAD: Cash available for distribution

Subject & References	Basic Attributes
Investing (Coxe 30)	What follows is really only a single attribute, specific to commodity investing, but I found this insight intriguing, and maybe you'll make some money as well, so I included it here. The attribute is that if you want to predict future metal commodity prices, you should look at current scrap metal inventories (apparently these are inversely related). "In our experience the behaviour of scrap prices is, quite often, a more reliable indicator of future metals prices than the action in spot prices for pure metals on the exchanges ... From our experience in talking with Midwest scrap dealers, they are among the first Americans to hear when China is changing its policies about economic stimulus vs. restraint ... Since the Industrial Revolution, the constraint on sustained metals price gains has been the supplies of scrap from products sold in earlier cycles."

Subject & References	Basic Attributes
Job Interviewing (1) (Schachter B6)	According to Sam Geist, a business consultant, here are ten key hiring questions. The rationale: these questions separate weak from strong candidates using these targets: Is experience described in general (weaker) or specifics (stronger candidate)? Are responses more about "what" happened (weaker) rather than on "why" it occurred (stronger)? Do candidates analyze failure, but not recognize their role (weaker) or do they analyze failure & success while recognizing their role (stronger)? Are candidates less self-aware of strengths & weaknesses (weaker) or able to accurately judge these (stronger)? 1. What was your most challenging job? Why? What did you learn from this job? 2. What was your least challenging job? Why? What did you learn from this job? 3. In what situation did you find that you had to overcome major obstacles to meet your objectives? What did you do? Why? What did you learn from the experience?

Subject & References	Basic Attributes
	4. Who do you admire most? Who do you admire least? Why?
	5. In what situation did you attempt to do something, but failed? Why did you fail? What did you learn from this situation?
	6. Describe a bad experience that happened to you. What did you learn from it?
	7. Describe a situation where you tried to help someone, change. What strategy did you use? How did the situation end?
	8. Describe a mistake you made in dealing with people. What did you learn from it?
	9. What was your best learning experience? What was your worst learning experience? What did you learn from each of them?
	10. Describe the last major change you made. Why did you do it? How did it work out? What did you learn?

Subject & References	Basic Attributes
Job Interviewing (2) (Veruki 48-142)	Of the 250 most common job interview questions in the reference, here are the top ones I ranked: 1. Passion for the Business: Why do you want to work in this industry [as opposed to just getting a job anywhere]? 2. Motivation & Purpose: Why should I hire you? 3. Skills & Experience: Tell me about a time you didn't perform to your capabilities? 4. Creativity & Leadership: Describe a time you had to alter your leadership style (cf. situational leadership; leading is not monolithic); 5. Compatibility With The Job: What interests you least about this job? 6. Personality & Cultural Compatibility: Describe your personality beneath the professional image; 7. Career Aspirations: What achievements have eluded you? 8. 50 Zingers: Tell me about a project in which you were disappointed with your personal performance.

Subject & References	Basic Attributes
	9. 50 Zingers: How have you handled criticism of your work?

Subject & References	Basic Attributes
Medical Diagnoses	Here is a series of questions for patients to ask doctors to refine diagnoses: - Replay: When no clear diagnosis exists, the patient can suggest to the doctor: "[May I] tell the story again as if [you'd] never heard it – what [I] felt, how it happened, when it happened?" (*How Doctors Think* 261) - Fear: If you are really afraid of what the diagnosis might end up being, ask: "[May I] tell [you] what is really frightening [me]?" (*How Doctors Think* 261) - Alternatives: If repeated tests still are inconclusive: "What else could it be?" (*How Doctors Think* 263) - Multiple Issues: If the doctor seems to be stuck on one (incomplete) diagnosis, ask: "Is it possible I have more than one problem?" (*How Doctors Think* 263) - Inconsistency: "Is there anything that doesn't fit?" (*How Doctors Think* 263)

Subject & References	Basic Attributes
Organizational Assessment (Drucker and Collins xii)	These are the top five questions to assess the state of a business in order to bring transformation: - Mission: What is our mission? - Customer: Who is our customer? - Values: What does the customer value? - Results: What are our results? - Plan: What is our plan?
Process Design Consulting (Work Plan) (Strachan and Tomlinson 166-167)	Questions for Developing a Work Plan: - Resourcing Adequate: "Are key stakeholders comfortable with the resources required to achieve the purpose and objectives?" - Milestones Achievable: "Are the milestones in the plan well situated, appropriately timed, and achievable?" - Logical Flow Confirmed: "Have the stakeholders each confirmed the logical flow of the work plan from their perspective?" - Commitment To Implementation: "How committed is your client to the implementation phase …?" - Accountability Promoted: "How does your work plan promote accountability for outcomes?"

Subject & References	Basic Attributes
	▪ Outcomes Achievable: "Are the outcomes for this initiative deliverable within the phases and time lines of the plan?"
Sleepover Questions For Parents (Arrington 15)	Questions to ask before permitting your child to attend a sleepover: ▪ Familiarity: Do I know the parents? ▪ Supervision: Will a parent be there? ▪ Agenda: Are activities planned? (scheduled events reduce mischief!) ▪ Attendees: How many children are invited? (check the adult-to-child ratio) ▪ Backup Plan: Do you know that I will be available? (let your child know in case they become anxious)

Subject & References	Basic Attributes
Sports Concussion Assessment ("Sport Concussion Assessment Tool 2")	NHL star Sidney suffered a concussion in 2011 which has prompted great interest in the proper way to assess potential concussions at the scene of a collision. The author states: "After watching in horror as Mr. Crosby was felled by a mammoth blow, lay on the ice, dropped his mouthguard, stumbled to his feet, skated hunched over to the bench and then returned to the ice, possibly with a brain injury – who could possibly think their sons or daughters will be protected after absorbing a similar blow in youth sports? All youth coaches from now on should carry … the SCAT2, or Sport Concussion Assessment Tool 2 … Don't ask an athlete who has been knocked silly, 'Are you okay?' Sidney Crosby and any 12-year old will say yes" ("Consider This"). SCAT2 includes these assessment questions: - "Ask where the game is being played." - "Ask what month it is." - "Read a string of numbers, ask for it in reverse order." - "Ask athletes to stand with bare feet together, hands on hips, eyes closed, for 20 seconds."

Subject & References	Basic Attributes
Talent Development (Colvin 118)	Geoff Colvin, Sr. Editor at Large, Fortune, posits that anyone can develop talent through "deliberate practice", which involves a variety of techniques including being able to observe oneself during the practice. "The best performers observe themselves closely. They are in effect able to step outside themselves, monitor what is happening in their own minds, and ask how it's going. Researchers call this *metacognition [italics added]*– knowledge about your own knowledge, thinking about your own thinking. Top performers do this much more systematically than others do; it's an established part of their routine." • Some of the questions that one asks oneself during metacognition: - "What abilities are being taxed in this situation?" - "Can I try out another skill here?" - "Could I be pushing myself a little further?" - "How is it working?"

Subject & References	Basic Attributes
Venture Capital (VC) Funding	Here are my own observations of what a VC investor looks for in a potential software investee: - Exit potential up to 10x investment. - Ability of the team to deliver is as important as the idea. - Preference to invest over two to three rounds. - Tendency to replace or bolster founders with professional managers after the first round. - Desire to syndicate (bring in other partners to pool capital) to spread risk. - Insistence on a patentable idea for intellectual property and investment protection.

Chapter 19

IMPROVING YOUR APT-ITUDE

The Questioning Lifestyle

We have covered a lot of ground in this book. By now you should be raring to go! You've seen the fifteen APT Principles up close and I hope the anecdotes have helped you to see how the Principles can be personal. Your objective is probably not to try to meet with the Queen but whatever goals you do have, if you work on your attitude, preparation, and technique, you will be able to get further faster by asking good questions.

It is a good time to remind you about that old "can't see the forest for the trees" warning (which by the way is why jump starting with attributes is important). Improving your observational skills is not about applying a rigid method – the essence is to develop a *questioning approach to life*. This was an underlying quality in Leonardo da Vinci and in the other experts from whom we have drawn in this book. That push, that drive to learn, to discover, and to get somewhere is the spark that will keep you on the front edge.

I once read an account of a seminary professor, Dr. Howard Hendricks, who exhibited this lifelong passion for learning. He would be invited to countless parties which often drew people together in polite, artificial, inane conversation – how many times do you want to discuss the weather? Not so with Dr. Hendricks. He would sidle up to a complete stranger and ask "What have you been reading lately?" Inevitably, a much more stimulating dialogue would ensue, setting up the conditions for good questions, good answers, and an exchange of ideas. I often apply his approach at social gatherings and I am the better for it.

Ask questions judiciously, but at the same time with some abandon too. You should have a pinpoint objective but spread a wide net to best capture what you will need to reach that objective. And do not worry about asking "dumb questions" – but at the same time, do not ask *obvious* questions. These drive students over the edge all the time. For example, suppose you are teaching ten year olds about gravity and then at the end of class you ask the question "So if you drop a ball from your hand what direction will it travel?" If the students give nonsense answers (like "up") or actually start to act up do not blame them – you are inviting bad behaviour by insulting their intelligence. Obvious questions have obvious answers that are a waste of time and add zero insight.

Pay attention to the basic attributes of a subject (whether there are six or not) so that you have a foundation to start asking questions. And when in doubt, you can always fall back on the most basic six attributes: who, what, where, when, why, how, the so-called "W5+H".

Remember that if you ask questions, then someone else is answering questions, and this is meant to be a give-and-take bilateral conversation. Author Max Lucado advises that we should also be aware that often, the first question we are asked is not the real question anyways. Hence, when answering questions, we need to probe for what is behind the questions. Mr. Lucado explains: "... a person's first question isn't really the question. Their first question is kind of like tossing the tennis ball into the air. It's a practice swing. They're just testing to see if I am listening to them or not. So I make a habit of following up the first question with a question of my own: 'Can you give me an example of that? ...'" (Dyck 26).

Tough It Out

Finally, if your objective is to learn something, then you must be ready, willing, and able to ask tough questions. In a recent newspaper article, *Don't Shy Away From The Tough Questions*, Wally Immen shares the following advice:

"People avoid asking them [tough questions] because they don't like confrontation ... but they can be the best way to get valuable information" (Immen).

Mr. Immen quotes Julia Alexandra Minson, of the University of Pennsylvania's Wharton School: "Everybody tells managers it's important to ask lots of questions. But even really bright people are uncomfortable asking probing questions that may result in negative response, so they only ask general and indirect questions that allow people to just skate around problems" (Immen).

Ms. Minson adds: "To draw out the information people would rather conceal, 'you have to be willing to ask negative questions that directly indicate that you believe there must be problems and you want straight answers'" (Immen).

And finally: "An example of a question that would elicit the information you want, she said, is 'I don't want to hear about how wonderful this is; tell me what really ticks you off about this'" (Immen).

Chapter 20

PUTTING IT ALL TOGETHER

Connecting The Dots

Time for one final look at the APT Principles:

FIGURE 20-1 The APT Principles

A ATTITUDE	Be Curious Be Creative Be Persistent Be Thorough Be Skeptical
P PREPARATION	Have A Specific Objective Do Your Homework Know Your Audience Choose The Right Person Don't Assume
T TECHNIQUE	Watch Your Language Listen Actively Soften Up Your Audience Ask Short Simple Questions Look for Inconsistencies

As I have mentioned many times now, the APT Principles do not operate in a vacuum, they are interrelated. One principle will lead into another one. Below are just some of the relationships that naturally connect up the various principles:

TABLE 20-1 Relating the APT Principles

APT Principle 1	APT Principle 2	Relationship
Be Curious	Listen Actively	If you are curious, you will want to listen attentively to the responses to your questions.
Be Creative	Have A Specific Objective	Being creative means identifying "the box" and devising questions to take you outside the box to someplace new – that "someplace" is your objective.
Be Persistent	Choose The Right Person	In my examples on choosing the right person it is clear that you do not often find that person the first time. Navigating through a network of contacts takes time and perseverance – you have to be persistent.
Be Thorough	Do Your Homework	If you work at becoming thorough then you will naturally want to do all the homework you can because you are focused on getting every last detail.

APT Principle 1	APT Principle 2	Relationship
Be Skeptical	Don't Assume	Being skeptical means that you will not accept information at face value – you will question the authenticity, accuracy, and relevance of the information to expose any assumptions that would mask what you are really searching for.
Be Skeptical	Look for Inconsistencies	Similarly, a skeptical attitude will drive you to compare information that you have unearthed from asking questions to assess if the information holds together consistently. That skepticism will aid you in finding inconsistencies, which often lead to a different path to better results.

Putting It All Together 247

APT Principle 1	APT Principle 2	Relationship
Know Your Audience	Soften Up Your Audience	If you know to whom you are addressing your questions, then you will research that person's background. The profile you come up with will lead you naturally to understanding what values or "hot buttons" to broach to create a bridge with your audience for your questions.
Know Your Audience	Ask Short Simple Questions	As you get to know your audience, you will learn what questions are the best ones to ask, and which ones not to ask.
Know Your Audience	Watch Your Language	Knowing your audience is clearly important as it appears here often. Another benefit of knowing to whom you speak is that you will be able to choose your vocabulary appropriately to build credibility and to open the door with the right words to be able to probe to where you want to go.

My Six Basic APT Principles

All fifteen principles are important and I urge you to learn them and practise them all well, including connecting them together the way they naturally relate and work hand-in-hand, back-and-forth.

But from my own experience (and probably due to my personality) there are some principles that I turn to more naturally. You will also gravitate more to certain principles for similar reasons. If I had to pick my "go-to" principles from each APT segment to always have at-the-ready they would be the following:

TABLE 20-2 The Author's Six Basic APT Principles

Six Basic APT Principles	Explanation
Be Curious	I think I naturally see things differently than most people. Call it a lack of common sense! But where people see obstacles I see possibilities.
	Imagination is a core value for me. If a child is reading a book set in the days of the Roman empire I'll ask what colour sandals are being worn by the characters. I'm glad there's a resurgent interest in reading among the younger crowd. Exercising the imagination is foundational to developing curiosity.
	Being a left-brained person I do track to certain details – I'll challenge myself when walking on the street to look at car license plates to see if there are any interesting patterns. I mentioned at the outset that I'm a stair-counter.
	I'm also a driven documenter – probably due to a deficient memory. Whatever the reason, documenting forces me to observe more, and writing things down enables reflection – all keys to curiosity according to Leonardo daVinci.
	Without curiosity, questions lose their raison d'être. An insatiable curiosity will formulate questions that others never think of.

Six Basic APT Principles	Explanation
Be Persistent	Since I am not particularly gifted with stellar brain power (nor athleticism), I had to learn to compensate. Persistence allows me to out-work others who are naturally better at things than me. Coming from a restaurant family, hard work was extolled and modeled by my parents, aunts, and uncles. Most immigrants could give us a lesson or two on the grit of perseverance, of not giving up nor giving in. To get somewhere on the backs of your observational skills and questioning abilities is not a "slam dunk". People will say "no" more than "yes". In fact, I expect resistance, so I'm never surprised when I encounter it. But I do not like to give up. Getting answers to incisive questions takes hard work to see them through. There's also a big payoff to persistence done right – when the going got tough in a startup we'd always tell ourselves "well, if it was supposed to be easy then everyone would have done it [our business] by now".

Six Basic APT Principles	Explanation
Have A Specific Objective	I find it challenging to take on any task if I don't know why I'm doing it and how it fits into the bigger picture. Purpose is the key to retaining the will to make the effort. It is said that people need to know "why" before they know "how" – I agree completely. If you are leading a team, it is the objective that must be instilled over and over again so that when setbacks deflate the team, they will fix their eyes on the purpose and find another way to meet it.
Do Your Homework	Similar to persistence, preparing by doing homework is natural for me. There is a wealth of data freely available to those who know where to look. Mining and leveraging that data makes your objective more attainable. There may be situations where snap decisions need to be made and risk incurred, but for the most part, homework can and should be done to maximize return on all your observation efforts.

Six Basic APT Principles	Explanation
Choose The Right Person	It takes more time to find that "right person" but it is worth it. Navigating through a network of people is usually necessary, but until you are dealing with the person who can address your questions, you are just sifting. I don't like to waste my time nor waste someone else's time, so I've become increasing blunt (while still being polite) in my quest to get to the right person.
Watch Your Language	Language is an ambassador that opens doors for deeper dialogue. I learned from my father to try to make people feel welcome and validated and to do so, you have to use the terminology that your audience is used to. I always want to build bridges, but to do so requires something in common that binds you to your audience – common language is one such bridge. Cultural values are embedded in language, so to smooth the way for your questions to get answered, the questions needed to be correctly phrased.

By this point I hope that you are beginning to see how many of the APT Principles converge to work together.

Ask The Extra Question

My wife bought a blender recently to make smoothies. If you've never had a smoothie, you should try one – there are lots of food stands around that combine fruits and even vegetables ("green smoothies" – an acquired taste) into a healthy vitamin-packed beverage.

The problem is, you need a pretty powerful blender to make a proper smoothie, especially if you plan to throw ice into the recipe. A good durable blender will set you back more than a few dollars. Because we had been scouring all the local health food stores for this particular make and model, I had a good idea of the market price range. As it turns out, my wife found a much better deal online so she put in the order.

Me? I had to ask the *extra question*. Why is this vendor selling the blender for such a low price?

You might chalk this up to being skeptical, or curious, or thorough. You might see this as part of doing your homework. I agree it is all these things.

The necessity to "ask the extra question" is really not a sixteenth APT Principle, it is a synthesis, a summation, the *epitome* of all the APT Principles. It is fitting to end this book by singling this out. I sometimes think of the "extra question" as the "question of last resort" - when you get stuck don't give up - ask the extra question.

So about our smoothie blender ... we later found out that the prices were discounted because the vendor was selling his business. It required an extra question to tease this fact out but possessing the answer allowed us to proceed with a purchase that I otherwise would have vetoed for fear that we were being sold a knock-off or a refurbished product.

When whatever you have set as your specific objective seems to slip from your grasp, when despite all the creativity, thoroughness, and persistence, and regardless of how much homework you did, no matter how you've searched for the right person and softened him up with simple questions – when you have tried every APT Principle and you "hit the wall" – do not quit - that's when you turn to the extra question.

Near Death Before Birth

Hitting the wall is a common occurrence in business, and especially at the software startup that I have mentioned a bunch of times in this book. The beginning of our company foreshadowed the kinds of desperate challenges we would face on a regular basis. We had a hot new idea in the field of database technology but needed to validate the idea and identify the right business partner to take this to market. Using my rule of working with the number two player (see the earlier chapter *Preparation – Don't Assume*), I thought about IBM, which had the number two database behind Oracle. To boot, IBM's development team is based in Toronto, so we would have better chances of building a deep relationship.

It took me a few months of persistence, creativity, and doing my homework, but I finally gained the interest of a senior product manager. He flew in for a meeting where we explained to him what we were working on and he showed great interest. However – all our hopes were totally deflated when he disclosed that there were other software teams at IBM that were working on solving the same problem we were targeting. He went on to talk about other resources associated with IBM that we could try to connect with to continue our work – I did not hear much of what he was saying as I felt we were done and he was just trying to let us down gently.

Putting It All Together 255

He had a plane to catch and was getting up to leave. As the whole short life of our little startup flashed before my eyes, desperation set in. Somehow, at that moment of crisis, the *extra question* came out: "If we could show a prototype solution to prove that our idea really works in the next few weeks, would he reconsider working with us?"

I had no idea if we could deliver in such a short time, even with the extraordinary team we had assembled. But amazingly, the IBM product manager agreed. Now all we had to do was build a prototype in less than a month! Our team delivered.

No Vacation Hideaway

Once I was debriefing a sales person after a customer meeting. I asked as I always do for some details to get a sense of how the meeting went. The sales person may have prepared and felt that he executed his entire game plan – but something was left out. I was told that the sales process was moving along well, that a customer showed interest and that we were asked to call back in a month when a specific IT executive would be back from vacation. The sales rep dutifully logged this information in the sales database and rated it as a sales opportunity with the action to call back in thirty days.

It all seemed reasonable - except to me. Thirty days could be never. Maybe I am too skeptical, but I saw a classic "brush off" in the making. In actuality, all the sales momentum being so optimistically reported could have fizzled out and the deal might be good as dead. How were we to know?

We needed to ask the *extra question*, like "Who is standing in for this vacationing executive and can I meet with him *now*?" If the response to that is negative – that there is no one standing in (highly unlikely), then I would ask if I could stop by to say "hello" to the executive's administrator. Why? You never know what you might learn from talking to an administrator (and in my experience, the administrator is the "gate keeper" to accessing an executive; the administrator knows a lot more than you may think).

Another extra question I would ask? I would ask where the executive is vacationing. You can call that "small talk" but you never know if that extra question will yield significant information in future.

Maybe it's your turn to be skeptical. What possible use would we have for knowing where our wayward executive is vacationing? Well, in the case of our software startup, I learned that seemingly insignificant questions about location would prove to be critical.

Hotel Check Out

Within five years of closing the first round of venture capital, we realized the dream of every startup – we were being acquired by a publicly traded technology company with over a billion dollars in annual revenue that needed our software to fill a strategic need. During the due diligence period that lasted several months we were coming down to the final strokes when we hit the most unlikely of walls - our property lease.

The landlord of the building that we leased is an international traveller with one of his residences in Europe. Our acquirer demanded signoff from the landlord on some legal papers and we could not find him – he was on a flight back to Europe. That is all his administrative staff would tell us. The missing signoff was not a trivial matter – the army of lawyers working on the closing had drawn up all the final documents for a specific date. If the date shifted, the all-important net asset value would need to be recalculated and the documents including government filings all revised.

I remember the crisis well. I have never been under so much pressure in my entire life. Going through the birth of our children was a "walk in the park" by comparison. I was getting calls from our Boston head office every hour. Everyone was waiting on me. The acquirer had more people working on this acquisition than the total number of employees in our whole company. My instructions were to try to reach the landlord every hour throughout the night. It was a virtual dragnet operation.

What did I do besides tear out what little hair I had left?

I asked the *extra question*.

I found out what hotel the landlord typically stayed at in Hungary, which is where he was headed. I called this hotel just to see if he was due to check in (he wasn't). So I called other hotels in the area - same response. I tracked down the landlord's son who was away at university just in case I needed his help. I asked the landlord's Toronto staff for the name of someone, *anyone* in Hungary who worked for him. I called that hapless Hungarian relentlessly until we were able to extract that final signature.

We missed the closing date by one day, but it was close enough. I am certain we would have missed the date by many more days with more punitive outcomes if all that pressure had not been applied. We only closed when we did because of that *extra question*.

What else can I say? The extra question is a summation of all the APT Principles, and in asking the extra question, you are embodying more than a methodology, more than a philosophy – you are embracing a way of life. Training yourself to "never say never", to never give up, to dig in and come up with that "one more" question will serve you well.

If your objective is important enough, you will stick to the principles, you will not throw in the towel, you will bob and weave and start putting out questions that are "outside the box". I cannot guarantee that your extra questions will always lead you to your objective, but you have to be relentless. From my experience, you just might be able to turn things around. Is it worth the effort?

Ask the Queen yourself.

Epilogue

WHAT HAPPENED WITH THE QUEEN

Lows from the High Commission

"Not yet." That was the news I received from the High Commission. As I learned three-times over, if you want an invitation to the Queen's Garden Party, you must apply through the High Commission. Your fate is entirely in their hands.

The letter I wrote, the photo I sent, the book I mailed, the correspondence and phone calls with the Palace, the Governor General, Canadian Heritage, and the High Commission – these all brought me to the front of the line – I believe that because of the responses I received from Lady Susan Hussey, from the obvious scrutiny of my package to the Queen, and from the increasingly warm correspondence from the High Commission (I am on a first name basis with the High Commission as well I should be since I've been tracking there for over one year now).

The problem with being at the front of the line is that there *is* a line. And since this year (2012) is the Queen's Diamond Jubilee, royal watching has hit fever-pitch, almost becoming an Olympic sport itself (and to further compound matters, the Summer Olympics really are in London this year too). In fact, precisely due to the Diamond Jubilee and the Olympics colliding, the Palace decided a scant one month ago to reduce the usual four Garden Parties down to two. Those odds I quoted earlier on getting invited? Just add a few more zeroes in front.

As you have seen them chronicled in my lengthy quest, the APT Principles certainly work – they are based on the broad shoulders of the many varied true-blue experts we have met throughout this book. However, even the full weight of fifteen tried-and-true principles on the backs of pit-bull Mike Wallace and company cannot penetrate a random lottery.

"Random" – I've come to revile that word. Teens love to use that term so *randomly*. Typical dialogue with a teen:

[Me] "Who gave you that ticket?"
[Teen] "Some random guy."

So this is the reality I now face. The High Commission has become a casino and invitees to the Queen's Garden Party will be selected not on merit, not on relationship, not on effort, not on determination but by *lottery. Random lottery.*

"Not yet." That is the message I received two days ago. I will have to wait another year to try to meet the Queen. It will not be the Diamond Jubilee then. But the Queen will be one year closer to beating the all-time record of sixty-three years on the throne held by her great-great-grandmother, Queen Victoria. There will still be enough pomp and circumstance to go around, I am sure. When I get to the Palace I will save you a cucumber sandwich. I owe you that much for sticking with me.

I hope you have found the quest worthwhile so far. As for me, has it been worthwhile?

Unquestionably.

Bibliography

Abagnale, Frank W. *Catch Me If You Can*. New York: Broadway Books, 1980.

---. *The Art of the Steal*. New York: Broadway Books, 2001.

Arrington, Candy. "Sleepover Savvy." *Thriving Family* Mar.-Apr. 2011: 15.

Baker, Katie. "The Timetable: Sidney Crosby's Lost Year." *Grantland*. 28 Sept. 2011. 30 Nov. 2011 <http://www.grantland.com/story/_/id/7023310/sidney-crosby-lost-year>.

Barker, Larry, and Kittie Watson. *Listen Up*. New York: St. Martin's Press, 2000.

Bone, Diane. *The Business Of Listening – A Practical Guide To Effective Listening, Revised Edition*. Menlo Park, CA: Crisp Publications, 1994.

"Canada's Food Guide." *Health Canada*. 3 Dec. 2011 < http://www.hc-sc.gc.ca/fn-an/food-guide-aliment/basics-base/1_1_1-eng.php>.

"Choose Your Cruise." *The Globe And Mail* 21 Jan. 2011. 21 Jan. 2011.

"Churchill Seeks Support From Roosevelt." World War II Today 30 Nov. 2011 <http://ww2today.com/8th-december-1940-churchill-seeks-support-from-roosevelt>.

Clairmont, Susan. "Cancer imposter pleads guilty to fraud." TheSpec 2 Nov. 2010. 1 Dec. 2011 <http://www.thespec.com/news/local/article/272402--cancer-imposter-pleads-guilty-to-fraud>.

Colman, George. *Cross-Examination – A Practical Handbook*. Cape Town: Juta & Co. Ltd., 1970.

Colvin, Geoff. *Talent Is Overrated – What Really Separates World-Class Performers From Everybody Else*. New York: Portfolio, 2008.

"Consider This." *The Globe And Mail* 21 Jan. 2011: A:1.

Cortez, Donn, and Leah Wilson, eds. *Investigating CSI, An Unauthorized Look Inside the Crime Labs of Las Vegas, Miami, and New York*. Dallas, TX: BenBella Books, Inc., 2006.

Coxe, Don. "The Metals Take Center Stage." *Basic Points* 1 Feb. 2011: 30.

"CSI: Crime Scene Investigation (season 1)." *Wikipedia* 2 Nov. 2011 <http://en.wikipedia.org/wiki/CSI:_Crime_Scene_Investigation_(season_1)>.

Davies, Nicholas. *Queen Elizabeth II, A Woman Who Is Not Amused.* New York: Carol Publishing Group, 1994.

Drucker, Peter, and Jim Collins. *The Five Most Important Questions You Will Ever Ask About Your Organization.* San Francisco: Jossey-Bass, 2008.

Duhatschek, Eric. "Crosby: Doctors working on techniques to take Guesswork out of Diagnosis." *The Globe And Mail* 20 Jan. 2011.

Dumont-Le Cornec, Elisabeth. *Wonders Of The World – Natural And Man-Made Majesties.* Paris: Editions de la Martiniere, 2006.

Dyck, Drew. "Glad You Asked." *Leadership Journal* Summer 2011: 26.

EduGuide Staff. "Types of Learning Styles." 29 Nov. 2011 <http://www.eduguide.org/library/viewarticle/2094/>.

"Elisha Gray and Alexander Bell Telephone Controversy." Wikipedia 3 Nov. 2011 <http://en.wikipedia.org/wiki/Elisha_Gray_and_Alexander_Bell_telephone_controversy>.

"Frank Lloyd Wright." *Wikipedia* 2 Nov. 2011 <http://en.wikipedia.org/wiki/Frank_Lloyd_Wright>.

Frost, David. *Frost/Nixon : Behind The Scenes Of The Nixon Interviews. 1st ed.* New York: HarperCollins Publishers, 2007.

"Garden Parties." *The Official Website of the British Monarchy* 30 Nov. 2011 <http://www.royal.gov.uk/RoyalEventsandCeremonies/GardenParties/Gardenparties.aspx>.

Gelb, Michael. *Think Like Leonardo da Vinci – Seven Steps to Genius Every Day.* New York: Delacorte Press, 1998.

Gladwell, Malcolm. *Blink – The Power of Thinking Without Thinking.* New York: Little, Brown and Company, 2005.

"Glenn Curtiss." *Wikipedia* 3 Nov. 2011 <http://en.wikipedia.org/wiki/Glenn_Curtiss>.

Greenspan, Stephen. *Annals of Gullibility – Why We Get Duped And How To Avoid It.* Westport, CT: Praeger Publishers, 2009.

Groopman, Dr. Jerome. *How Doctors Think.* New York: Houghton Mifflin Co., 2007.

---. Dr. Jerome. "Your Doctor and You – Why Doctors Make Mistakes." AARP Magazine Sept. & Oct. 2008: 34.

Hardman, Robert. *A Year With The Queen.* New York: Touchstone, 2007.

Harris, Richard. *The Listening Leader.* Westport, CT: Praeger Publishers, 2006.

Hartley, Gregory, and Maryann Karinch. *I Can Read You Like A Book.* Franklin Lakes, NJ: The Career Press, Inc., 2007.

Immen, Wallace. "Don't Shy Away From The Tough Questions." *The Globe And Mail* 27 July 2011: sec. B:15.

"Invention of Radio." *Wikipedia* 3 Nov. 2011
 <http://en.wikipedia.org/wiki/Invention_of_radio#Marconi>.

"Iran Hostage Crisis." *Wikipedia* 30 Nov. 2011. <
 http://en.wikipedia.org/wiki/Iran_hostage_crisis>.

Isaacson, Walter. *Steve Jobs*. New York: Simon & Schuster, 2011.

Jarvis, Carolyn. *Physical Examination & Health Assessment, First Canadian Edition*. Toronto: Elsevier Canada, 2009.

Josephson, Allan M., and John R. Peteet. "Talking With Patients About Spirituality and Worldview: Practical Interviewing Techniques and Strategies." Psychiatric Clinics of North America 30, issue 2 June 2007: 181-197.

King, Larry. *Larry King, My Remarkable Journey*. New York: Penguin Group (USA) Inc., 2009.

Lawrence, Shawn. "Samuel Weiss: Science and Serendipity." Bioscienceworld 3 Dec. 2011
 <http://www.bioscienceworld.ca/SamuelWeissScienceandSerendipity>.

MacKinnon, Gordon P. *Investigative Interviewing*. Mississauga, ON: Old Village Press, 1996.

McLaughlin, Paul. *How To Interview – The Art of the Media Interview*. North Vancouver, BC: Self-Counsel Press, 1986.

"Mike Wallace." *60 Minutes* 1 Dec. 2011
 <http://www.cbsnews.com/stories/1998/07/09/60minutes/bios/main13549.shtml>.

"Milestones: 1937-1945." *U.S. Department Of State, Office of the Historian* 30 Nov. 2011 <http://history.state.gov/milestones/1937-1945/LendLease>.

Newhart, Bob. *I Shouldn't Even Be Doing This! – And Other Things That Strike Me As Funny.* New York: Hyperion, 2006.

Nicholson, Nigel. *The Queen & Us.* London: Weidenfeld & Nicolson, 2003.

"Pablo Picasso Quotes." *BrainyQuote* 30 Nov. 2011 <http://www.brainyquote.com/quotes/authors/p/pablo_picasso.html>.

Pepper, Ian K. *Crime Scene Investigation – Methods And Procedures.* Maidenhead, Berkshire, England: Open University Press, 2005.

"Post-It Notes." *The Great Idea Finder* 4 Dec. 2011 < http://www.ideafinder.com/history/inventions/postit.htm>.

"Q & A with Nigerian Scam Con." *Marketplace* 1 Apr. 2011 <http://www.cbc.ca/marketplace/2011/wontgetfooledagain/nigerianscam.html>.

"Real Estate Investment Trust". *Wikipedia* 27 Nov. 2011 <http://en.wikipedia.org/wiki/Real_estate_investment_trust>.

Riedl, Sue. "Dear cheese diary, today I'm a little blue." *The Globe And Mail* 18 May 2011: sec. L: 3.

"Right Brain vs. Left Brain Creativity Test." *The Art Institute of Vancouver* 1 Dec. 2011 <http://www.wherecreativitygoestoschool.com/vancouver/left_right/rb_test.htm>.

"Robert H. Dennard." *Wikipedia* 29 Nov. 2011
    <http://en.wikipedia.org/wiki/Robert_H._Dennard>.

Ryan, Andrew. "The Next Testy Brit for Americans to Adore." *The Globe And Mail* 11 Jan. 2011: sec. R: 4.

Schachter, Harvey. "Ten Must-Ask Job Interview Questions." *The Globe And Mail* 3 Jan. 2011: sec. B: 6.

"Scott Adams." *Wikipedia* 3 Dec. 2011
    <http://en.wikipedia.org/wiki/Scott_Adams>.

"Sidney Crosby." *Wikipedia* 30 Nov. 2011
    <http://en.wikipedia.org/wiki/Sidney_Crosby>.

Sismondo, Christine. "A Royal Tradition." *The Globe And Mail Report On Business Magazine* May 2011: 83.

"SplashID Password Manager for Mobile Devices, Mac OS & Windows." *Splash Data* 10 Nov. 2011
    <http://splashdata.com/splashid/worst-passwords/>.

"Sport Concussion Assessment Tool 2." *Sport Alliance* 4 Dec. 2011
    <http://www.sportalliance.com/index.php/component/docman/doc_download/45-scat2>.

Stafford, Tim. "The Foot-Washers of Ethiopia." *Christianity Today* May 2011: 54.

"Standard 52-card Deck." *Wikipedia* 30 Nov. 2011
    <http://en.wikipedia.org/wiki/Standard_52-card_deck>.

Strachan, Dorothy, and Paul Tomlinson. *Process Design – Making It Work*. San Francisco: Jossey-Bass, 2008.

"The Frustrations of Fra Mauro: Part I ." *Apollo 13 Lunar Surface Journal* 4 Jan. 2006. 4 Nov. 2011 <http://next.nasa.gov/alsj/a13/a13.summary.html>.

"The Guests." *The Official Website of the British Monarchy* 30 Nov. 2011 <http://www.royal.gov.uk/RoyalEventsandCeremonies/GardenParties/TheGuests.aspx>.

The Innovator's Toolkit – 10 Practical Strategies to Help You Develop and Implement Innovation. Boston: Harvard Business School Press, 2009.

"The Role of the Sovereign." *The Queen's Diamond Jubilee* 31 Jan. 2012 <http://www.2012queensdiamondjubilee.com>.

"Upper Canada College." Wikipedia 2 Dec. 2011 <http://en.wikipedia.org/wiki/Upper_Canada_College >.

Veruki, Peter. *The 250 Job Interview Questions You'll Most Likely Be Asked … And The Answers That Will Get You Hired!* Holbrook, MA: Adams Media Corp., 1999.

Wallace, Mike, and Gary Paul Gates. *Between You And Me – A Memoir*. New York: Hyperion, 2005.

Walters, Barbara. *How To Talk With Practically Anybody About Practically Anything*. New York: Doubleday & Company Inc., 1970.

"What Happens At A Garden Party." *The Official Website of the British Monarchy* 30 Nov. 2011 <http://www.royal.gov.uk/RoyalEventsandCeremonies/GardenParties/WhathappensataGardenParty.aspx>.

"Woman of the Bedchamber." *Wikipedia* 1 Nov. 2011 <http://en.wikipedia.org/wiki/Woman_of_the_Bedchamber>.

Woods, Michael, and Mary B. Woods. *Seven Wonders of the Ancient World.* Minneapolis: Twenty-First Century Books, 2009.

Woods, R.S.M. *Police Interrogation.* Toronto: Carswell, 1989.

"29 Dimensions of Capability." *eHarmony* 28 Nov. 2011 <http://www.eharmony.com/why/dimensions>.

"3 Steps For Choosing A Child Safe Organization." Commit To Kids 28 Nov. 2011 <http://commit2kids.ca/pdfs/C2K_ParentCard_en.pdf >.

"52-Card Deck." *Wikipedia* 5 Nov. 2011 <http://en.wikipedia.org/wiki/Standard_52-card_deck>.

ABOUT THE AUTHOR

Albert Lee is a technology entrepreneur and business strategy consultant. He has held various senior posts (President, CEO, Board Director, VP of Business Development, Head of Sales & Marketing, Chief Strategy Officer, COO) in over twenty-five years in the software industry.

Mr. Lee co-founded a software startup, xkoto Inc. in 2005, raising $10 MM in venture capital. xkoto received numerous awards including the *Deloitte Fast 50 Companies To Watch* (2006) and *Information Week Startup Of The Year* (2008). The startup was acquired by Teradata Corp. (NASDAQ: TDC).

In 2010 he founded the Nilwall Group to provide strategic consulting in governance, business development, sales, and marketing to technology firms. He sits on the Advisory Board of SWI Group.

From his technical training, business successes (and numerous failures), and volunteer work with children, Mr. Lee lives and breathes a passionate conviction that better observation improves every pursuit.

He has been volunteering for over ten years in his local church to teach children how to make better observations, developing his own curriculum that draws on his business experience and belief that we all need to observe better by asking good questions.

About The Author

He has spoken at numerous industry events including IBM's *Information on Demand*, The 451 Group's *Enterprise Summit*, the *Canadian Investor Forum*, the *Next Generation Data Center*, Microsoft's *Worldwide Partner Conference*, and Vancouver *SQL PASS*.

Among his academic achievements are the following: three-time city-wide public speaking champion, two-time graduating class valedictorian, student body president, Dean's Honours List distinctions, recipient of an Imperial Oil Research Scholarship and a National Sciences and Engineering Research Council Scholarship. He earned an Honours B.Math degree from the University of Waterloo and a M.Sc. degree from the University of Toronto.

To reach Mr. Lee, send email to author@6basix.com or visit www.6basix.com.

Made in the USA
Charleston, SC
02 January 2013